# AN AMERICAN
# NIGHTMARE

## THE STORY OF SCARY MOMMY
## AND THE SEX OFFENDER

BY LOUELLA THOMAS

# AN AMERICAN NIGHTMARE

## The Story of Scary Mommy and The Sex Offender

## By Louella Thomas

*Cover Art by Zilla*

"The children early on wrote Monster on a piece of paper... and when I'd ask who that was, they'd say "Monster"....so that is how that name actually came to be, and it is fitting.

"Devil," the children said once when I begged them to tell Mommy and ask her for help (many many times) they'd say "Mommy's with the Devil," or "Mommy is the Devil." Sometimes they called Mommy, "Scary Mommy." Scary Mommy indeed.

This story is about that Monster and that Devil, who shall hence force be known as Monster and Devil. To me they have no right to a decent name. Decent people do not inflict hell upon children. Nor do they lie before a judge under oath for the purpose of terrorizing and inflicting pain upon children.

**What you are about to read is a true story. Only the names have been changed to protect the guilty.**

# Synopsis

Trying to encapsulate this story is so hard to do. Three little girls, who were left alone in this world, with no one to help them. Ignored by their mother, their mother's family, the father's family not listened to....no one cared. These are my beautiful little granddaughters, Layla, Emily and Annie. My son Mick's beautiful little girls, that we love to death, and haven't seen for almost three years.

Three little girls who were swallowed up by a sex offender and his awful friends, whom I'd rather call Monsters. Three little girls begging for help. Pleading their father, their Mim (me, their paternal grandmother), anyone who would listen.

Evidence of rape injuries, documented by an emergency room physician who is the head of the emergency department. A document that the sex offender can have no contact, and yet these injuries were ignored by the judge.

In every turn we took; DCFS, Judge, police, state representative, governors, the President, no one stopped to look at the truth, and help little girls.

These little girls were trafficked from Illinois, to Florida, Hawaii, Oklahoma, Brazil.....all the while against a court order. I found this information. Why couldn't the police and the FBI find it? Why didn't they care? And if I was able to find it on my facebook, why didn't they find it? Because they didn't care.

Because the insertion of the police who participated seemed to have a reason to make sure that Monster never paid for his grave disgusting actions. Monster's Uncle Ernie who is a cop, placed himself smack dab in the middle of this case, and lied and conspired to help the mother move the children to Monster. Everyone always made a clear path for Monster. And Devil Mother was always there to make sure that no one stopped him from raping her children. These little girls happen to be my granddaughters that

I love. I have to hear their pain, their cries, they show me their little bodies, turned inside out, swollen, broken, horribly distended, like a monkey's bottom. It's something I wish I'd never seen, and something that tells me quite graphically that these little girls are being raped, sodomized, tortured.

The girls begged and pleaded and screamed for help. Whenever they were with us, they would ask us why no one helped, ask our friends, and no help came. We sought help, but every time we met a brick wall.

DCFS initial consultation by Tracy Allen of Danville, assured us that the sex offender would have charges brought against him by nightfall when the girls told her of the sexual abuse they suffered. When she sent the report in, Kankakee DCFS said "it will be put in the file, when you asked the children where they were from, the grandmother said "Kan"....and that negates the rest of the interview." Excuse me. They went on to discuss a litany of sexual abuse done to them by Monster, and that's not noteworthy. And I said nothing. I sat quietly while three little girls told a litany of horrors done to them by a grown man, a sex offender!

On and on and on it went. Everytime we tried to make a way to stop their hell, Devil Mother would again, throw down her ace. Devil Mother stopped a two week safety plan against herself and Monster........think about that.....a safety plan against her for allowing her children to be raped by a sex offender.......she stopped it. The police came and took the children with no paperwork and stopped the investigation. Who's running the show here?

We have been harassed, threatened, knocked down, lied about....and its been horrific to bear. But the real hell has been upon three beautiful little girls, whose mother and mother's family, have conspired to have them live with a sex offender. They have lied and conspired to place three beautiful innocent little girls with a sex offender. My mind cannot ever take it in.

I love these little girls. I haven't seen them in over two years. My heart aches every day for them. Their father is living in hell knowing what is happening to them. We all miss them more than we could ever explain. We are miserable on a daily basis, but try to endure and last until the day we know that God will allow us to see them again.

I pray that in reading this book, you will realize what has transpired right here in America. Little children being trafficked and raped, by a sex offender, against a court order. No one listening. No one caring. No one helping.

It's a tragedy. And not one that little girls should ever have to endure.

This is 2012. This is America. Little children should be safe from a Monster and a Devil Mother. No child should have to endure this hell. Ever. Shame on all of us that this is happening in America.

If there is a God, and I believe there is, I am praying daily for this hell to stop, and I pray that as you read this book, you become as enraged, saddened, and horrified I am that this is happening, and please God, let it end.

God Bless.

# Table of Contents

# Dedication

I am dedicating this book to my son Michael Joseph Thomas, or Mick as we call him. He's a funny, sweet person, who loves his daughters as much as any father could. He adored spending time with them, and they with he. We miss them more than anyone could ever dream. I know he misses them everyday, and every hour, and carries a huge pain in his heart for his darling little girls. Their little faces, their laughter, their sweetness, their silliness, are qualities that we adored. I pray for the day that we see them again. I pray that they are surviving. I pray that they know how very much we miss them, and that one day they will find a peaceful, safe place to be.

I pray that Devil and Monster pay for what they have done to three, innocent, beautiful little girls.

**"There is no crueler tyranny than that which is exercised under cover of law, and with the colors of justice."**

-Anonymous

# Preface

On September 20, 2007 the court made an order that Monster Thomson could have no contact with the children. Their father had gone into the court and told the court about the claims the children made that Monster was molesting them.

My son's lawyer called up Monster's previous conviction 96JD118, and the Judge A ordered that Monster could have no contact with the children at all. The mother of the children could not live with the Monster.

On February 13, 2009, Dr. Kruzak testified to the rape injuries that were inflicted upon Emily and Layla by Monster Thomson. And Judge A did nothing to protect the children. Nothing.

What was the purpose of a court order that no one followed?

# Introduction

The great sadness that envelops me is more damaging than anything I have ever encountered in my life. To have to protect myself, as a grown woman, against monsters in this world, is something I feel fairly equipped to do. To have to try and protect little girls from a sex offender, while their mother, and her entire family serve them up, is something I can barely think about much less try to conquer. When these little girls happen to be my granddaughters, my son Mick's beautiful little girls, it is beyond heartbreak and despair. I often try to rationalize to myself which is more egregious; the events that are happening, or the fools that are allowing it to happen.

I have fought this battle at least four years with no one on my side, other than our immediate family and friends. All of the gendarmes, so to speak, have all protected the sex offender. It's been absolutely horrific.

I never dreamed something so horrific could take place in my United States of America. I have doubted my country before but upon this occasion I am dumbfounded, and eternally ashamed. I am saddened beyond despair that the contributions my family has made to this country do not mean anything. We have been threatened, chased, arrested, tormented, and lied to repeatedly by the authorities. No one has helped at all.

We are supposed to be the strongest country in the world, but one of our greatest tragedies, is that one of the most flagrantly violated laws in this country, is child trafficking. And no one cares. Lots of voices I hear on my television, and often read in the newspapers about someone being arrested. But I don't see anyone going after the monsters. Our local authorities and the authorities where the children are being trafficked, will do nothing. NOTHING. We have been chastised by authorities for calling too often to see if anything has been done. There is no heart for little girls who are suffering at the hands of a vile monster.

My granddaughters are being trafficked by a repeat sex offender. And no one in the local government, nor the state government, not the national government has helped stop the hell against these children. I have been told by many government officials that this is a local matter. No its not a local matter. I have read all the web sites that discuss trafficking children. My granddaughters are being trafficked. From Illinois, to Texas, to Brazil, to Hawaii, to Colorado, to Florida. This sex offender has taken these little girls across many states lines, and national lines, all the while against a court order. And no one will listen and no one will help.

I owe a big debt of gratitude to Marilyn Van Derbur, a former Miss America, whose book I read, and who carried me through some very rough days with words of wisdom and words of encouragement, and who forever knew and felt my pain. I hope she realizes that her ability to share what she survived gives me hope. I hope and pray my granddaughters survive. I know that she went through her own personal hell to become whole, and I applaud her for everything she's done for herself and for others.

And to my good friend Cyndi Chadwick, who suffered this abuse herself as a child, and was always there for me, to bolster me up, to hear my voice, and to often go back to her own pain and sorrow as she helped me through the darkness. In her voice, and in her words, I don't think she realizes how much comfort and wisdom she has given me. To both of these strong women, I owe a debt of gratitude. They both survived and thrived. Despite the people who hurt them and terrified them. I have to say, that I know from my granddaughters, its such a deep, ugly, scary place to be. It is not anything I really fathomed until I had to face it. Children being hurt in anyway is a tragedy. Having innocence and trust taken, is unforgivable. Think of your own childhood. Your own fears. The boogy man has come to life, and he's in your house, terrorizing you. Little innocent children. What mother lets that happen?

And to my beautiful granddaughters, Layla, Emily and Annie. You are three of the most beautiful, strong and wonderful girls I

6

have ever known. Little girls who delighted in everything that was done for them. Playing outside, picking flowers, riding bikes, helping me make dinner, laughing, being silly, just being little girls. You tried so hard to tell what was happening to you, and to get help. The fact that your mother chose to lie, and subject you to this hell, is something she will have to deal with as you grow up and realize how badly your mother deceived you. Deceived her darling little girls so she could have a sex offender in her life. Not caring for the cost to her beautiful little girls. May you have every blessing and prayer that I can place on you. I pray for your strength to overcome everything that has been placed on your little shoulders.

My family, especially my son Mick, the girls father, for putting up with me, as all of us were and are so very distraught at the pain and suffering that these little girls have been made to endure, and still endure at the hands of this monster. My son has had to bear the weight of his little girls being raped, repeatedly by this monster and the monster's disgusting friends.. The monster's name is Monster Thomson. And he is a sex offender. From here on out he shall be Monster, because that's what he is. He's a Monster who devours little girls. And his girlfriend/wife Devil shall be called Devil, because she is the Devil who hooked up with him, and decided to let her children be devoured, She knows the truth. She has seen their private parts, bulging, bleeding, broken, filled with semen. I have seen this, so I know she has seen it as well. They have been sent to us for visitation looking raped and broken. Who does that?

She chose to lie in court, and traffick the children across state lines and national boundaries, for the sex offender to have his prey. She actually stated on facebook, "I love you baby, it is almost done." This was a few days before she went into court and lied for the sex offender. Which she gladly did repeatedly.

May God shine a light one day upon these beautiful little girls and help them to safety. They are beautiful sweet little girls. It all began when Layla and Emily, identical twins were about a year and a half old, and when Annie was a baby. We began to see and hear things that made us fear this was true. One day the girls broke their silence and it all spilled out in horrific detail.

To say its been a horrific journey would be the world's greatest understatement. It's been a hell that has terrorized me, my husband, more than anyone, my son Mick, their father; our other two sons, Beau and Ted, our other beautiful granddaughter Candi and our friends who have been destroyed by this Monster and Devil trafficking the children.

The authorities have the nerve to tell us its local. No, when you traffick children against a court order all over the globe, its federal. It's a federal offense to take children across state lines for the purpose of raping them, and allowing others to rape them. My responses from the White House has been that this is a local matter. No, trafficking children across state lines is a federal matter. He has also trafficked them to Brazil, which makes it an international crime. Maybe one day when adults who are responsible for the safety of children in this country, take that pledge seriously, this horrific story would not have to happen. I have to live with that hell everyday. I can name so many people who for reasons that are unclear to me, have allowed these little girls to suffer in this horrific situation.

I pray in writing this book that something changes. That someone listens. That someone cares..

I am very saddened that my country, America, is allowing this to happen. When I was growing up, we always loved our country and felt we were the best, regardless of what anyone else believed. I am currently ashamed that my country allows this to happen.

Child trafficking is one of the largest crimes in this country.

Let's all see to it that this changes. Please. For the little ones, the broken ones, the sad ones, the children that have no help. Please help me make this change. Little children should matter to all of us.

# Chapter 1 - Please allow me to introduce myself

Beginning this story is daunting to say the least. My beautiful little granddaughters, Layla, Emily and Annie have been with their mother and her sex offender boyfriend/husband for at least four years. It is heartbreaking. My son Mick is their father. He had been married to their mother Devil, whom I shall call Devil for obvious reasons. They were now divorced. She had an affair with one of his best friends, who killed himself, and was now firmly entrenched with Monster.

Layla and Emily are almost 9 year old twins, and Annie is 7. We haven't seen them for over two years. Didn't even know where they were for over a year. And it was a year of hell. Not knowing where they were, but knowing they were in hell, placed there by their lying mother Devil. We live in Illinois where the children lived before their mother took them away. With lies. All she knows how to do is lie. Our fears eat us alive. We are all terrified because we know what the fate is. Their fate is hell.

It all began for us on April 29, 2007 on my son Teddy's birthday. The girls had come to our home for the weekend and to celebrate Teddy's birthday. They loved Teddy to pieces. They would chase him and jump on him, and laugh and laugh. I got up early and drove to Champaign to pick him up. When we got back home, all three girls were outside waiting for him. They ran for the car, laughing and screaming and yelling his name. It was a wonderful familiar moment. Whenever they saw anyone in our family, they would run and scream and jump into their arms. At that time of Teddy's birthday, Layla and Emily were 4 (identical twins) and Annie was 3. Precious little girls.

They spent a lot of time with us. Almost every weekend. Often from Thursday until Monday. They played and watched tv, and cooked with me, (they could make a Chicago style pizza that would knock your socks off) and laughed and went to the library, and drove their little car around the house and rode bikes. It was a very magical time.

However Ted's birthday took a very unexpected turn that has forever since left us shattered. It has now been at least four years ago. We came into the house after Teddy played outside with the girls for an hour or so. We were all going inside to relax a little while, and I was going to start cooking dinner. In a very quiet moment, Emily put her hand in front of her, and said from nowhere, as if in the Twilight Zone "Sometimes Monster takes his fingers like this, and puts them in my chachi (vagina).....and sometimes he has a long fingernail and it scratches me and it hurts". I felt my world start to turn slowly in my head......I closed my eyes, and prayed to myself "I didn't just hear that....dear God she said something else". But I had indeed heard it, as she began to speak again. "And he reaches into the bathtub when we're taking a bath, and puts his fingers in our chachi, and we have to rub his bat". I felt my head start to turn towards Teddy, like an axis going round the earth, in slow motion. The words she spoke were as if a tape recorder had slowed them down.........As my head was turning, I felt Teddy's head turn towards me. Both of us were staring at each other with our eyes about to pop out of our heads. And to my utter panic and pain, we had indeed, heard this child say that she was being sexually abused. She continued on "he makes us kiss him, and he'll take his tongue and stick it into our mouths." Little tiny Annie, the baby, said from the couch "he pees on me". I turned to Layla, and she was literally fading away. She was off the love seat, standing and looking like she was melting. Her eyes were flooding with tears, and she pulled her hair from both sides across her face, and looked as though she wanted to disappear. Emily continued to talk "He comes in our bedroom in the night, while Mommy is snoring and he takes us out of bed, and into another room. Then he takes off all of our clothes and he takes his bat and pees on us. Sometimes he covers my eyes so I can't see. It's really scary. I don't like it." I felt as though every breath of air I'd ever thought of breathing, had somehow escaped me. I couldn't breathe. My heart was racing. I felt tears spring to my eyes. I was in shock. I was beyond shock. I didn't know what to say. I didn't know what to do. I honestly don't remember if I said or did anything while they told us of the horrors they had to endure. At one point my husband came in the house. I turned to him, and put my finger to my lips to let him know not to talk. He heard what the girls were saying as well.

They kept talking. Emily and Annie for awhile. It was gut wrenching. Layla barely spoke. Emily spoke a lot. Annie chimed in occasionally. Annie said "he puts me on the potty and he pees on me Mim." (the girls name for me). Layla looked like she was going to pass out. Her face was collapsing....she was almost crying internally......her face was covered by her hair, as she drew it across her face, with tears, but no sound. I will never forget the sadness that overcame her. I said to Layla 'Honey, let's go upstairs for a minute and talk." I don't know why I did that. I have no idea. I was befuddled and broken, and confused and horrified.......much like Layla........We went upstairs into my bedroom. I felt Layla needed a private moment to pull herself together. Why I walked away from Emily and Annie I don't know. I closed the door. I said "Honey does he hurt you?" She shook her head yes, and burst into tears. I said "Layla, I'm so sorry that someone is hurting you. You are a wonderful little girl. No one is supposed to touch you or hurt you. We'll get help. we'll tell Mommy, we'll find someone to help us. Mommy will help you." I saw the door open a crack and there in the hallway were Emily and Annie. I brought them into the room, and all of us sat down. I repeated my words to them. "We will get help. We'll tell Mommy. No one can hurt you. Nobody can hurt you girls. You are my darling little girls and I'll help you." Teddy had gone out onto the porch to smoke a cigarette and cry. Not such a happy birthday after all. His little princesses were being hurt, and it really hit him hard.

As if her antenna were up, in that very moment, the phone rang. It was their mother, who for reasons that will become very clear to you later, I call Devil. She said to me immediately "what's wrong?" I said "You can't imagine what these girls are saying to me." I did my best to get all the words out, and she told me that if this was true, she would kill the son of a bitch. (her words) The son of a bitch is Monster Thomson, Monster. Because that's what he is. He's a Monster, who has raped and defiled little girls. My beautiful little granddaughters. My little girls. My son's little girls.. My darlings. Their childhoods stolen, broken and bruised. Their little bodies being defiled. Fear. Pain. Anguish. Not knowing what in the hell to do next. Why is this happening to them? Unbelievable angst and pain. I later learned that my greatest pain would be trying to imagine how this horror could be processed for three little girls. My knowing that they had to endure this hell caused me more anguish and pain.......because the pain wasn't inflicted upon me. A grown woman who could fight for herself. The pain was inflicted upon tiny little girls. By a Monster. Who in truth is nothing but a coward.

Devil, Devil, said if this was true, she would kill him. He'd have hell to pay if this were true. We made plans to meet the next day and talk. The girls and I went downstairs and went on with our day. I felt like I was out of body. I was shocked into silence. I so wanted to tell Mick their daddy. But I was afraid. Shocked. Never heard anything so disgusting in my life. My brain couldn't begin to process it. I trusted that Devil would handle it. What a mistake that was. Huge mistake. For this mistake I will always carry great guilt for what might have been. I have had to face that guilt many times when Devil has thrown down her trump cards. Devil always found a way to one up me. Cunning. Like a fox. I had felt she would stop this monster from being with my granddaughters. Her daughters. But no. Not to be.

The day was strange. I was lost. I was making wok chicken. I have a huge wok and I'd fry up all sort of veggies and then fry up lots of chicken, combine it all and serve it over rice or noodles. I didn't realize til I was cleaning up that night, that I'd made a big pan of chicken and a big pan of vegetables, and never made rice or noodles. I couldn't function. I didn't function properly for probably a month. The thought of someone harming my little girls, and nothing being done about, it nearly drove me insane. It is a feeling that still lives in me. These darling little girls are still being molested by Monster, and Devil allows it. She has stopped every investigation we have, she lies, she threatens the children, Monster threatens the children, and the terror and molestation goes on. The girls have been through investigations, and Devil stops every one of them. She likes her children being molested. It's a horrifying thought as a grandmother to know that your little babies are being raped on a continual basis. It never stops. Never stops.

I digress. We drove Teddy home that evening after everyone left. It was as though a horrific move had played earlier in the day and we hadn't yet recovered. My son Mick did not know that they told us. I was in shock. Deep shock. Sadly, I had believed Devil would hear this story of horror and help her daughters. "Get out of here, I never want to see you again. If you ever come near me again I'll call the police." Didn't happen. Jesus was I dumb.

When we got home that evening after taking Teddy back home, Mick said "Layla waited up for you. She wanted to tell you something." I saw that precious little peanut passed out on the couch. "She only fell asleep about ten minutes ago. She really wanted to say something, but she couldn't stay awake." I felt my heart break. I loved these little girls so much. I had them about four or five days a week since Annie was a baby. Mick and Devil had divorced when Annie was really little and Devil was a slut, drunk, drug addict. So we had them often. Usually every Thursday through Monday. So they were a very real part of my life. To know that they were being molested and physically damaged was really more than my heart could take. When my children were little, as most mothers, I doted on them. Kissed and cuddled them. Made sure that every little aspect of their life was perfect for them. And this bitch devil, was allowing a Monster to devour her children sexually. Babies. They were only babies.

The next morning when they got up, I was beside myself with grief, to have to take them home. I didn't know what to say or do. My son Mick did not know still. I couldn't bring myself to tell him. He had so many crazy things happen since his divorce and split from their mother, Devil. He was so vulnerable. I really believed that Devil would fix this. I really believed. This was a major learning lesson for me. Once you are a Devil, you are the Devil. She had shown herself to be vile and despicable so many times. Why would I believe there was anything good left in this Devil?

Joe, my husband was playing with the girls. Emily and Layla went by the front porch and sat with Papa. (Joe) Papa said "you think everything will be alright?" They said "No". We finally loaded up the car. On the way I was so positive. "We'll tell Mommy, she'll help us. Remember to tell her everything you told me. I know she'll help you. She loves you so much.' Annie thrust out her forearm and fist defiantly and her legs straightened in her little car seat, and she blurted, defiantly and strongly, "Don't worry Mim (their name for me).....I be strong." I turned around, faced the road, and tears poured down my face. All of my fears started raging in me. I tried to calm myself. I prayed. I cried. Again, my stupidity made me believe that the mother, Devil, would help these little girls. Her little girls. I forgot. I was dealing not with a Mother, but with a Devil. A Devil who sold out her babies, to a child molester, and did not care.

We got to the park, where we were to meet Devil. It was about forty minutes from my house. I almost went back home about 10 times on the way. We waited for Devil for almost forty minutes. It was over 100 degrees out. She knew the girls had something they needed to tell her about, that it was really sensitive, and they needed her help. She made us wait forty minutes. When she finally did arrive, I realized very quickly that she did not care at all. When I told her what the girls had said, Layla started to cry, Emily ran away, and Annie blurted out "he pees on me Mommy"........all she said was "Monster doesn't hurt you, he'd never hurt you. He loves you. He'd never hurt you. Big Poppy loves you.' I immediately said "Who in the hell calls themselves Big Poppy?" She wasn't hearing a word. Nor was she asking any questions. Because she knew all the answers. I learned it in one minute of being with her. She knew. She didn't care. Any mother worth her salt, would say to the girls, "Come over here. Sit down, and tell me what you told Mim. Does Monster (Monster) hurt you? Is Mim telling me the truth?" No, she began her sing song of the same thing that she must have repeated at least a hundred times........."You know Big Poppy loves you, he'd never hurt you. He loves you girls. He'd never hurt you. He loves you. He'd never hurt you." Over and over and over. Never asked one question. Just kept singing the same old tune. It took about two months for my brain to scream at me one day "she's part of the abuse.' I sort of thought so, but her refusal to even hear the story, tells volumes. I would have sat my kids in front of me, and said "tell me everything you told Mim. I will help you. No one is going to hurt you. Tell me." And then allowed the children to speak. No. She filled every moment with her song......blah blah blah. Didn't want to know. Doesn't want to know.........pretend.....pretend.

Talk about the Devil. Please allow me to introduce myself. I'll never forget my son telling me that the first time he had sex with Devil, that he looked up and saw her head tossed back, and saw the devil in her face. Yes indeed. We were now with the Devil. My little granddaughters were in the land of Devil and Monster. Talk about your world crashing down. Bricks and mortar all around me. And I felt it. I felt like the world had dropped onto me and I couldn't move. I cried. I couldn't sleep. I couldn't concentrate. I couldn't read. My brain would just go back to the moments when the children told me what was happening to them. And I knew that they had no safety net. No one would help them.

Unbelievable. Gut wrenching. I came home, and tried to tell my son. I was barely in the house for a few minutes, when the phone rang. It was Devil. She said to my son Mick. "The girls are fine, Monster didn't do anything. I took Layla to the doctor, and he said she's fine. Monster didn't do it. And if you say anything again, I'll say you did it." (This threat was a very real threat. One we reported to police, but no one ever acknowledged. Several months later she coached Annie to say that Daddy molested her. Protecting Monster by lying to her children! What kind of lesson is this for a child!) He hung up the phone and looked at me like he'd been shot. He told me what she had said. I then had to delve into the nightmare that my granddaughters had told me. I was so horrifically sad and hurt, and distraught that I hadn't told him. The shock and anguish had killed me. And I did the wrong thing. I should have told him. But I feared he would panic. The girls had told us previously that Monster , Monster, was very mean to them. Hitting them, pulling on their arms, yelling,.........and it upset him terribly. I thought Devil would care about the molestation and stop it.. I couldn't have been more wrong. More lost. I tried to apologize. I tried to tell him

I hoped for such a different outcome. I tried to find a way to stop the pain. God help us. God help us all.

My life had changed in a moment. In that moment when the girls divulged what was happening to me, I had become aware of the fact, that my little granddaughters, my babies, were being sexually molested. I had many moments in my life, that I really thought had been horrific. But this moment, this story of pain upon my babies, was absolutely the worst. I couldn't breathe. I couldn't think. I couldn't begin to understand how something so horrific could be happening. I cried. I cried. I couldn't stop crying. I had hurt my son. My granddaughters were in danger. Being raped. Often I think of rape victims that go through this horror once, and wonder how they survive. Now I had the knowledge that my granddaughters were being raped on a regular basis. The monster was in their life. Welcome in their life. By a Monster. And their own mother, the Devil, Satan's spawn, would do nothing to stop it. She loved the sex offender Monster. Her entire family loved him. He was a welcome Monster in their lives……..my heart, my mind, my soul……….seemed to all fall to pieces. Just falling to pieces……Never in my life had I had such a conundrum.

My sides hurt, my heart hurt, my head hurt. My arms ached. My thoughts burned my mind. I could not imagine this grown man, big man, doing this to my little babies. I could barely breathe. I could not think. Thinking made me cry. I tried not to think. Not to feel. Then I would realize that everything I felt was just my fear for them. When I had to process that everything I felt was merely my angst for them, I had to realize that the real horror and pain laid upon the souls, hearts and bodies of three little girls. And I mean little. At this time, Layla and Emily were going on 5, and Annie was 3. When I had to realize the pain was on these tiny girls, I would just about die. This pain was ten fold for my son, their Daddy. He loved these little girls with all his heart. They were his babies. For him to have to know that a grown man, a very sick man, a pedophile, was given carte blanche to do whatever he wanted to his baby girls, it was deafening in its intensity. It was a pain no man should ever have to face for his children. It was ripping out his soul. I knew why I hadn't told him. It made no

16

rational sense. It was stupid.. But the old saying "kill the messenger" holds true. But I came to realize that I couldn't process the pain.....and neither could he. We were both in Hell's Kitchen........these were our precious little girls. However, I realized, that I had taken from him, the chance of handling the situation on his own.. And the guilt floods in. The guilt lives with me every day. Will always be a source of pain for me. In thinking somehow I could spare him from pain, I inflicted more pain. A sadness that will never leave me. A sadness that will stay with me forever.

The girls and I and Devil at the park. In the heat. Melting. The girls wanting to have their mother help them. Devil gleefully saying over and over like a mantra "Monster loves you, he'd never hurt you"....All the while my mind is saying "That's love?" I finally lost my nut, and had to leave. I said "Please help these children. If you don't we will have hell to pay one day. They're suffering. They've come to us for help. Help them." I got in my car and drove away. Empty. Sad. Defeated. Knowing she would do nothing to help. As I drove away, she and the girls were swinging, talking as though nothing had happened. Just another day at the park. She did not help them. She went home to Monster that night. The girls back in Monster's house.

God help me. I had never encountered anything so disgusting in my life. And this horrific incident, was happening to people that I adored and cherished more than anything in the world. My granddaughters. My sweet darling girls.

Devil held the girls from us for three long months. We missed them terribly. If we called they wouldn't answer. She always had an order of protection against Mick, so he couldn't go to her house.

We knew the Devil had been unleashed, and she had the reins on the girls. And she gladly relinquished them to the Monster.

# MONZTER STORIES

I wanttostop
my chachi hehurt

toDaD

toMor

monster

NONO!
he hurt these
PeoPle Name
E
L
A

19

Mom

21

**Pictures of Layla, Emily and Annie**

I have pictures the girls drew of their hell for their psychologist Dr. Judy.

They are sad beyond sad for three little girls to be drawing. The twins were 7 at the time and Annie was 5. They were pleading for help. This had been ongoing for over four years.

It's very interesting that Monster Thomson called the psychologist, that he refused to have an interview with to regard his safety factors in regards to living with the children, in conjunction with making a threatening phone call to her, that she said "if" she interviewed him it would have to be at a secured building with bodyguards. But the courts saw to it that he was with the children, who were offered no safety from this Monster.

Dr. Judy wrote to the courts, that she was the person who was hired to evaluate the safety of Monster Thomson as a person the children could be with.....and that she had very serious regards with this issue.

I quote:

> **In November 2008, I completed a custody evaluation on behalf of the three children belonging to Michael Thomas and Devil Mazur: Layla, age 7, Emily age 7 and Annie age 5. I have been provided with a copy of a petition to modify custody submitted by Devil Mazur, which would appear to created a risk of harm to the three Thomas children. In her petition, Ms. Mazur has stated that she intends to have a relationship in the future with Monster Thomson and stated that he has never been adjudicated a sexual offender. According to an order filed 9/20/07, it was reported that Monster Thomson is an adjudicated sex offender and subsequently he was precluded from contact with the three Thomas children.**
>
> **In conducting my custody evaluation on behalf of the three Thomas children, I requested the opportunity to evaluate Monster Thomson which was not allowed. Subsequently, in the custody evaluation I completed, I recommended that Monster Thomson complete a comprehensive psychosexual evaluation prior to any consideration for contact with the Thomas**

**children. In consideration of his status as an adjuciated sexual offender, it is critical that a qualified expert evaluates Mr. Thomson to determine his potential risk of harm to the Thomas children prior to any consideration that he has contact with the children. Without Mr. Thomson's completion of a psychosexual evaluation by an expert with a report provided to the Court, the three Thomas children, Layla, Emily and Annie, would be considered at high risk in his presence.**

**Respectfully submitted,**

**Dr. Judy**

I had sent this letter with the court order to a few people I saw on facebook, that were his friends, who obviously had small children that they spoke of and had pictures of on facebook.

I warned them of his previous conviction, and that my granddaughters feared him greatly and that he raped them. I also sent a copy of the court order so they would know I was serious. I was stupidly, as a grandmother, thinking these people would care and be thankful to know that a friend of theirs, was, indeed a sex offender.

The most amazing response I received was from a nurse, who told me if I contacted her again, that she would contact the police and have me arrested. I told her to have at it, as we were used to the police being threatening and cruel and doing nothing.

Also on June 22, 2010, in response to my doing the above, Monster Thomson called Dr. Judy and left a voice mail on her office phone in Champaign. The following is in a letter that Dr. Judy sent to the courts. " He stated that he lives with Devil and the three Thomas girls stating "I take care of his kids.....send them to school, to the doctor." Monster said that Mick is sending the letter I had written concerning him (Monster) to Monster's friends and family in which Monster stated "I continue to be abused by him." In addition, Monster said that Mick had been arrested two weeks ago. Monster asked me to call him . Due to the circumstances of this case and my lack of current involvement, I did not return a call to Monster."

I love it. He's court ordered to have no contact. He is a sex offender, who trafficked these children across state lines, across international borders, called the father and said "I rape them, I'll continue to rape them, they're my kids,",.....and my son is abusing him! Ah......insanity......a sex offender, who also happens to be insane.

Also on June 22, 2010, Dr. Judy sent me the pictures that I have included, that I had not seen until she sent them. They are the pictures these darling little girls drew for her......if that isn't sadness.....I don't know what is.

I am totally confounded day by day at the insanity of what has happened to these little girls. That a dirty sex offender, can traffick them about the globe, with the full complacency of the police, the courts, everyone.

Sad day. Sad day indeed.

As a very sad aside, in the past few weeks, I've been going through old documents and letters trying to make sure I haven't forgotten anything and that I've covered all the bases. I found, much to my sadness, and complete shock, the add by Judge A, and Legislator Lisa, where they are walking together on a nice day, with trees around them, smiling and advocating......In Juvenile and Family Court Judge A has shown her main concern is the protection of our children. Rep. Lisa is supporting Judge A on November 4th because she knows that Judge A understand the important work of looking out for children in the 21st century.

Neither of you did one thing for a child. Neither of you cared one iota for what happened to these children. You both turned your back and purged yourselves of any responsibility and let three little girls pick up the tab, for a frickin sex offender. Are you kidding me? You people have lost your minds.

Who do you turn to? Where do you go?

You don't. Little children are at the mercy of these people who have the complete pass from judges and representatives, who are too lazy or too stupid to do their jobs.

# Chapter 2 - Hell is for children

The days that followed the revelation from the girls, were horrific. I couldn't sleep. I couldn't think. I couldn't really do much of anything. I would burst into tears at any given moment. I had to have a picture of the girls next to me, that I would rub with my thumb until I cried. My heartache for my little girls was a larger pain than anything I'd ever experienced in my life. My chest hurt, my sides hurt, my heart ached, I cried, sometimes sobbing, everything in me hurt. My mind could only keep asking 'why, why is this happening to my little girls?"

The mother made sure we couldn't see them. They were kept from us. They were kept from us for a very long three months.

My son, their daddy, Mick and I went to the police. My neighbor and police officer, who is also a very nice family man, set up a meeting for us with the Bourbonnais police. Officer Milfred. It was gut wrenching. Something I never dreamed in my life I would be doing. Discussing the rape and horrors placed upon my granddaughters. I hate the word molestation. It sounds like you messed up your hair a little bit. It's rape. Rape. The police officer remembered my son. Mick had found pubic hairs in Annie's diaper a year earlier. Two long pubic hairs. She had just arrived at the house from Devil's with a wet diaper that had public hairs in it! He had called Monster's house and screamed in anger, "Keep your hands off my daughters, you keep your f&*$ing hands off my children." He called Devil and she laughed and said "I have pubic hairs in my pants too, we'd better call the cops.." The police man remembered that incident. My son indeed went to jail for nine days for that phone call. Devil had her usual and always order of protection (I think she's had them for over six years now, like buying gum, she signs up and they give them to her, with no evidence but her word). So Mick was arrested and placed in jail for breaking his order of protection. Never mind that he'd found pubic hairs in his little girls diaper. I believe at the time she was barely a year old. And the most heartbreaking, jarring part of this meeting for me was the police officer telling us a year later, the same police officer, that indeed Monster, the Monster, was a sex offender. 96JD118. It's a number that's burned onto my brain. From the first moment it was told to me, I have remembered this wretched number. Why didn't the policeman tell my son this story a year ago, when he came in because Monster, the Monster, had called to have him arrested. Monster took his voice message into the police and had my son arrested!!!!! No concern for the girls, then, now or ever. We were dumbfounded, as we remain.

I had to tell the policeman the story that the girls had relayed to us. I found myself just about retching trying to get the words out. My son left the room. It was too painful for him to hear. After I finished the story, I was sure that the policeman would go and arrest Monster immediately. They did not. In the next few days they took the girls out of Monster's house, where they were living with Monster and Devil, and moved into her mother's Shorn's (Devil's mother) house. Whereupon, Shorn and Floyd (Shorn's boyfriend) left for vacation the next day. So now instead of molesting the girls at his house, he would molest them at Shorn's. Perfect. What great planning. You could do nothing to stop Monster. Great planning by the police. Police basically doing nothing while a grown man, who has been labeled a sex offender, has his way with three little girls. Ditto, ditto, ditto. Never ending.

As I spoke with Lt. Milfred he reached behind him for a piece of paper. The mother, Devil had come to the police, and again, and requested an order of protection. Devil claimed that Mick saying the girls were being raped was a lie, we made it up, and she knew all about Monster's childhood conviction. He just hit her or something. This was also the crap we heard from Devil's lawyer. He stated in open court, that 96JD118, was merely a battery. He would later say that Monster merely battered his 3 year old half sister. Just roughed her up a little bit. That's not true, and frankly I don't want my granddaughters around a child batterer nor a child molester. They took the time to prosecute him, and convict him for molestation. Let's call it what it is. It's sexual abuse. We have been told many times, that it is a horrific story. Horrific. I would also like to add that the judge wrote that Monster was a convicted sex

28

offender on the court order. The mother Devil chose to have it change to adjudicated sex offender. Same beast.

Oddly Lt. Milfred became a protector of the Monster. Devil played a cat and mouse game with my son. She would call him to go have dinner with her and the girls, ask him to stop by, she'd drop by his place, all very friendly. Then when it was convenient she'd call the police, and have him arrested. I remember one Christmas, after they split up, she called on Christmas Eve and wanted my son to come up and spend the evening with her and the girls. I was leery. She has always had an order of protection. Going on five years at least…..and she has a trigger finger. She'll grab that phone and call the police the moment she's angry about anything. Not on the sex offender, on my son. So he gives me the phone and says "You talk to her." So I take the phone, and she says "It's Christmas, these are both of our girls, I think it would be a good thing." So he went…….and when he was there for a short little while, who shows up but Monster. Monster…….Mick said she just grinned like a Cheshire cat. And Monster ran. He ran and got in his car and took off. He's only a Monster against little people. Not so tough against grown ups. Mick said that he just thought "this is crazy", and got up and left. Games Devil plays.

So after the police report, the girls were taken by Devil into DCFS (Department of Children and Family Services) where they were questioned. We were told by Greg of DCFS, that each child had an adult with them. Devil was with Layla, Shorn was with Emily, and TJ was with Annie. Coverage. The room they waited in was miked, for the police to hear……..Greg and the police officer had to go into the room, and tell them to stop coaching the children. The adults (idiots) were repeating over and over "Remember Monster didn't hurt you, he'd never hurt you, you're fine, remember he didn't hurt you"……..the mantra had begun. Greg and Officer Suprenant ran into the room and said 'You can't coach the children", but they had. The interviews went on from there. They were too afraid to speak, although they said Annie, then 3 told them she couldn't tell what Monster does because then her Mommy couldn't marry him. But the damage was done. The damage is done routinely. They are not allowed to speak the truth. They know this very well.

The Bourbonnais police officer Greg Milfred became Monster's protector. Devil had her court order of protection for herself and the children against Mick. So if Mick drove by he'd be arrested. The most insane incident of all will never cease to amaze me.

The evening that Mick and I went to the Bourbonnais police to report the crimes by Monster against the children, I went and picked up my daughter in law, Angie, and Mick's then girlfriend, Brooke.. We were going out shopping and getting pizza for dinner. I had never known where Monster and Devil lived. So Mick gave me the address and we drove by on the way to get pizza. (Devil had never told us she had moved the children in with Monster. My son had followed her a few times, and knew that was where she lived.) Angie being silly, honked the horn, as if to say "we know where you live now sucker".......Monster and Devil were sitting in their front room, with a large picture window in front of the house. Devil and Monster starting yelling and freaking out, like in a ridiculous movie, and flipping us off. Had it not been for such a serious, horrific reason it would've been funny. They looked like a couple of rabid dogs barking and swearing at the window, shaking their fists and swearing.

Mick had earlier taken his truck and gone on to a friends. Mick gets a phone call from Lt. Milfred. Wants to know where he is and wants him to come to the police station and turn himself in. Mick asked him in complete amazement "what in the hell are you talking about?" The officer says Devil and Monster called and said you are driving by and harassing them, and her court order is still in affect. Excuse me. It was my car, not my son's car. My son then called me, and I was to go turn myself in or be arrested. I went to the police station, and went inside. I was very polite. I told the officer, "I was with these two girls, and we were just going for pizza and drove by.....and honked. Nothing happened. Officer Barney Fife looks at me, in his too small shirt and pants with his neck buttoned up so tight he looks like his head will explode. "You cannot go over there and antagonize these citizens." I said "I didn't antagonize anyone, we drove down a public street and honked a horn. There's no law against that." To which he replied, "Well Mam , I've warned you, they've called and made a complaint, and if you continue doing so, we will arrest you." I said "There's a sex offender there raping my granddaughters." Barney says "Ma'am that has been referred to the proper authorities, now do I have to tell you again."

Yes, putz tell me again. Tell me how a horn being honked at a sex offender is more egregious that a sex offender raping my tiny little granddaughters. He appears to weigh about 280 with his lard ass, and my little girls probably weigh 50.

Okay, let me dissect this. We go in and tell them that the girls say he's raping them. The girls are afraid. Little girls. He's a sex offender. They are to be investigating him. I felt they should have arrested him. But no. They are going to arrest me, for driving down a public street and honking my horn. Welcome to the police and law enforcement aisle. Don't pass go, do not collect $200. Get the hell out of Dodge. Raping kids…….no problem. Honking horn at sex offender…….huge problem. I was learning very quickly that the police are not my friend..

However, Lt. Milfred became Monster's protector. Lt. Milfred would call my son and ask him why his car was near Monster's house. My son said he'd look around, and he could see the police car a few blocks away watching him. My son would say "why are my girls with this sex offender and you're not doing anything." Mick would start his car up and leave. He'd park a few blocks away to try and see the girls with the sex offender, but rarely saw him.

The police never made a move on the sex offender. He was never arrested. We were told by a Kankakee police officer, where Shorn lived, that it couldn't have been Monster, because he didn't even live here anymore. He had moved to Oklahoma, and wasn't around the girls at all. Which to us was funny. Because Monster came from a wealthy billboard family, and could travel with ease.

Layla once stood in my living room and asked me why no one was helping the girls. They would often freak out on me, and want to know why no one would help. I told Layla "They say he's gone, and he doesn't live here anymore." I can see Layla right now in front of me, a little five year old full of spunk and frankly pissed off as hell, as she screamed "he flies on airplanes, he comes and he goes." Well Layla, you're smart enough to know that, but the police and the judge can't figure that one out.

I also had occasional outbursts from all the girls. One time, to my great sadness, Annie, then about 3 years old, climbed into my lap. She curled up and nestled into my body. She said "Mim will you help me?" I said "What's the matter?" Annie said "Monster hurts me Mim. Can you make him stop." I told her that she had to tell someone, because no one would listen to me. I've never felt lower and sicker in my life. And the one that rips my heart out, every time I have the memory........Emily and I were upstairs and she was playing.........all of a sudden she was talking and overcome with pain and sadness, and she started jumping with her little feet, and she cried, and said " sometimes they take me in a room, and they pull on my clothes, til they get to my under panties, and they pull them down my leg, and take turns…" …..and with that she fell on the floor and burst into tears. We occasionally had these melt downs, and they killed me. The mother and her family wouldn't hear of it. They wouldn't listen. In the psychologist's report, the girls told her that they'd tell their mother, about Monster, and they wanted help, and she would say "Do you want me to cut off all your hair? If you keep saying that I'll cut off all of your hair. Monster loves you." I try to imagine their little brains trying to process this. They'd often ask me "Can't somebody help us?" Or they'd say 'Why doesn't anyone care?' I finally had to tell them, "You have to tell someone when you're with Mommy. When you're with Mommy she tells you to lie, so she has everyone believing that its not true." They would get so angry. And this was what I lived with my granddaughters. For over two years, a desperate sadness, trying to find a way for little tiny girls to be able to speak up, when their mother and her family had all aligned themselves with the sex offender. What in this world could possibly be more disgusting? I have asked myself repeatedly that very question. What? Nothing. Absolutely nothing. Selling out little girls to a sex offender, for whatever reasons they had.......were frankly.........unbelievably disgusting and revolting. Nothing lower in this world.

When the investigation by the courts began Monster moved. He moved to Oklahoma, and had an address there. He moved about freely. He was in Florida, Oklahoma, Kankakee, Illinois, wherever he chose to be. So since he was mobile, he couldn't have been in Kankakee, if you believe the police in Kankakee. The biggest bonehead of all was a detective in Kankakee. Etzel...the head of child endangerment. I remember his name, because they were Etzel and Chrysler...cars...Etzel asked the girls if Monster molested them. They were with their mother. Who loves the sex offender. They said No. If you ask once, then that's it. We told him, that the girls were being repeatedly molested. And he was just 100% sure that if they tell more than once, it isn't true.

Well every time I see the girls, they tell me something that is happening to them. So I guess they're liars. The twins are almost four and the youngest is almost three, and they're just making all of this up!!! Little girls lying and telling me sexual abuse horror stories for no damn reason. All three of them are hallucinating the same story. Imagine that. Quite a story these little girls have concocted. The Stupids are in Kankakee, and they're running the show. And of course the coup de taut........I made it up. That was Devil's family's story. We made it all up. If I was going to make up a story about my granddaughters it would be complimentary.......not some frickin horror story. And if I made it up, how in the hell did it turn out that I was indeed correct; that he was indeed an adjudicated sex offender. I.E., plead guilty. He had a juvenile conviction at 17 for raping his three year old sister!!!

How many 17 year olds rape their baby sisters!

The horrors never stop. Welcome to my nightmare.

34

# Chapter 3 - The Addam's family

Trying to process Devil's family is something my mind has never been able to handle. To say they are weird or odd, is a blinding understatement. They think they are somehow the most important people in the world. Not in the area of having confidence or beliefs in yourself. In thinking they are better than everyone else. And they are not better than anyone. They are odd. Very odd. And hateful, and vengeful. And frankly, stupid. Really dumb.

What type of a family welcomes a sex offender into their family and doesn't question why that is happening. They threw all caution to the wind, and immediately welcomed him. The children didn't understand it. Neither did I.

When I first met Fern, the mother of Devil whom I shall call Shorn, I felt like I'd met a troll. A brain damaged troll. I'm not usually judgmental but this woman was odd. On her first conversation with me, on the phone, she told me she was a rape victim. She drudged through the details and told me all about it. I'd never met her! She went on and on and on. I later learned from a client of mine (I was a manicurist for years) that Fern had gone into local business meetings as a featured speaker and spent the time telling about her rape. These meetings were small, with maybe 25 local business people. The client was stunned, as the usual speakers usually covered crafts, or business ideas, or something enjoyable. She said it was the creepiest experience of her life.

I call her Shorn because she has her hair mowed at least every other week. She has a pompadour on the top of her head, and the rest is practically shaved. She looks like a man, and turns up her nose. Her boyfriend of many years is a barber and shaves her regularly. This barber I'll call Floyd (he looks like Floyd on Mayberry) lived with his mother til he was 60. Shorn disapproves of everything that is said, and has a superior attitude. My granddaughters called her "Grumpy" and "Grouchy"......in fact when the psychologist went to their house for the family interview

Layla told Dr. Judy straight up, that grandma is a grouch. Devil immediately blamed that on Mick, their father. Nice try. Layla knows of what she speaks. This woman, Shorn, was an impossible drudge. Just completely dismal. Layla knew of what she was speaking.

And Devil's father......what a painstaking sour puss this was. He weighed possibly 115 pounds, shaved his head, and wore jeans so tight they looked as though they had been painted on. And for that I call him Tight Jeans, or TJ. He languished around Devil like he was her lover. When they hugged, he would press his body together with hers, so they were flush from head to hips and they would hug and hug and moan oohs and aahs. It was really something nobody wanted to see. It did not look like a father hugging his daughter. It looked like a dirty old man squeezing a young girl. And I believe he was indeed a dirty old man. Devil had told Mick early on in their relationship that her father molested her and she had no relationship with him. Mick was very confused by all of it, but encouraged her to talk to her father and have him in their lives if possible. What a crushing mistake that was. Once the twins were born, TJ was up her ass. Up the girls asses. Just an obstinate source of irritation. Mick at the time worked in Chicago, an hours drive. When he'd get home, he'd want to spend time with his kids and relax. He'd lock the doors, and be inside playing with the girls. TJ would go to the front door, to the back door, and finally climb onto a second floor patio to get inside and see the girls. He was unstoppable. He felt these children were his. And he would force himself upon them whenever he wanted to.

TJ and Devil were also huge cigarette smokers. My son hated it when they would be in a car, with the windows up and the girls in the car, and they'd smoke. Sometimes both of them. The girls were constantly sucking up their cigarette smoke. They often had to have asthma treatments from breathing problems related to the cigarettes. My son told me that he once pulled TJ out of the car with the girls, when he pulled up in a car filled with smoke. These people were beyond belief. The things they would do were unbelievable.

36

To my point, TJ was with Devil all the time. He hovered over the twins. Thought he was their dad. (He and Shorn had a bad divorce and she had taken up with Floyd when Devil was a baby.) My husband and I went to watch the twins then one and a half, when Devil was pregnant with Annie. Devil had a doctor's appointment. My husband rarely went to their house, so going to see the twins was a wonderful experience. They had windows in the front of the house. The girls would stand on their little chairs in front of the window so they could see out. When they would see our car, they would go crazy because we were there.

We would probably have three hours to play with the girls. And we loved it. While I was there the phone rang. It was TJ. He wanted to know what was going on. I told him that Joe and I were watching the girls. He said "I'll be right there." And he was. He hung up the phone and drove straight to the house. When he came into the house, you could feel his presence. And it wasn't light. It was very dark. He would lay on the floor and grab the girls close to him, and hug them and kiss them. They wanted to play and would run and try to get away. When he decided it was time to leave, he gave one of the creepiest performances I've ever seen in my life. Lecherous. Award winning..........Emily had crawled into my lap, and Layla was in Papa Joe's lap. We were just sitting back and relaxing. TJ came in front of me, and kneeled immediately in front of me. His knees were pressed to mine. He took Emily's hand and began sucking her hand, smooching and sucking on her hand like an octopus, with a grip. The flesh of her little hand in his mouth. Almost sexual. Smooching and making noise and suckling them. All the while he was making noises like he was in ecstasy and bobbing his head around. He was so creepy looking and his actions were so vile......it seemed like an eternity......it was disgusting.......I turned to Joe to see if what I was feeling was really happening. Joe's eyes were bugging out of his head, and he was looking away in disgust. Layla's eyes were frozen, like she had been in this situation before. No expression, no faces, just frozen in fear and time. He got up after what was probably three minutes and went onto Layla. I remember turning to look at Joe several times in amazement, and damned if he didn't plop himself in front of Layla and do the same thing to her. Suckling her little arms. Smooching and kissing her hand. Rubbing her face and grinning like a Cheshire cat in a freaky movie. I felt maybe someone should check his pants and see if he'd ejaculated. That was how horrific it looked and felt. This grown man, in front of us caressing and suckling little girls was nothing anyone should ever do to a child. It was perverse. It was sick. I now know the apple doesn't fall far from the tree. It was one of the most revolting things I'd ever seen in my life. I thought he needed fifty bucks and a whore. Not little girls.

Little did Mick know when he had Devil reunite with TJ that Pandora's box had been opened. Never to be closed.

Back to Floyd, the barber. Floyd was an insufferable prick. He was right. He was always right. He felt that whatever he said was the way it was. He was short, about five feet tall, and fat and gross. He felt that he knew everything and things went his way. He'd shoot anything that he didn't like. Rabbits, squirrels, dogs. He had a huge pick up truck that looked like a building. For a little tiny man.

Floyd became a huge fan of the Monster, and defended him to the point of insanity. He once brought the police with Devil to pick up the girls at their Daddy's. The state police had called my son during an investigation, and were speaking to him saying they weren't finding any credible evidence. My son said "really, the girls are here, do you want to talk to them".....to which he put the phone into the air, and said to the girls "Tell this police man what Monster does to you." To which the girls all yelled "He hurts us, he puts his penis in us, we don't like him." Mick got on the line and says "did you hear that?" The police officer didn't care (imagine that, none of them do. The girls were never interviewed with their father, or anyone from our family. Only with the Devil's family who protected the sex offender, always.) Within a few minutes Devil and Floyd were at Mick's house to pick up the girls. It hadn't been his weekend, so she claimed ownership and took her kids. Mick had called her to tell her what the girls were saying. There were days throughout this hell that the girls would just spiel for hours of what Monster was doing to them. Mick would beg Devil to help the girls. And that was never going to happen. So Devil and Floyd came to claim their meat. The girls were yelling at Floyd that he was wrong. Floyd was pointing his finger, and blabbing "You're going to jail. I'm going to put you in jail." These people want my son Mick in jail. Not Monster. Mick. They don't have any of their paddles in the water. Certifiable.

As for the rest of Devil's family and friends: All pretty forgettable. Her best friend Eliza is a mirror of Devil. An absolute idiot. Couldn't fight her way out of a paper bag. Dumb as a box of rocks, we'll call her Rocksy, cause she is a box of Rocksy. She would write to Monster on face book "MTMTMT just wanted to say and that's what up!!!!" and my personal favorite of hers, that she wrote about my son, "Karma's a bitch MT!! This is what he gets….he fucks himself every time: I understand he makes you madder than mad, but everyone knows you're a good man." I never heard he was a good man. I heard that he's a convicted sex offender. As my friend Cyndi tells me 'Oxymoron'……and yes Rocksy is a moron as well. 96JD118. Monster's conviction number. I don't know where these people are getting their Kool-Aid. Devil's sister Mari, rhymes with Sorry, and Sorry she is. From here out we'll call her Sorry, if there's ever reason to mention her. There really isn't. She's drinking the Kool-Aid. She's a Vanilla Phosphate. Boring. Boring. Boring. Yet Sorry is in a picture on facebook with Monster, Devil and the children. So she too is happy to have the children with the sex offender, against court orders. Sorry, Floyd, Rocksy, Shorn, Devil and Monster, are raising my granddaughters. Monster rapes them.. And they all stand back and allow it. How can little children survive this life? How? The stupidity of these people and the situation my granddaughters are in is deafening. The idiots at the asylum (police, authorities, court) went with the mother, Devil, because she went to the courthouse first, she got the first, second, third, order of protection….God only knows how many she's gotten. She has them as her weapon against my son. You need no proof to get these pieces of paper. Just write down a bunch of crap on a piece of paper and away you go. Whenever my son gets angry and wants her to stop allowing Monster to be with the children, she gets an order of protection.

The first time we went to the police and filed a report about Monster raping the children, Devil got an order of protection on Mick to stay away from Devil, Monster, and the children. How? You walk into the courthouse, fill out the paperwork, and voila!!!! Order of protection!!! Her children were on an order of protection with a sex offender, who the children claimed was hurting them, against their father. The nuts are running the asylum!!!! And the scariest part for me, is once they take the side of the first party they hear from, you're done. God himself couldn't write a wrong. Eventually the judge learned the truth, but not in time to help my babies. By the time the judge pulled her head out of her ass, it was, and remains, too late. We were even told by my son's first lawyer, that the judge got sick of Devil's lying and finally left the case. Well why didn't she do something about it, and save the children from the hell that was their daily life!!!!

So very much has happened, that it is hard to keep it all focused and in perspective. The only real issue, is that these little girls are continuing to be harmed. That they were trafficked to Texas to live with a sex offender against court orders. That the mother, Devil and her family, Shorn, TJ, Sorry, all lied in court, to take the children not to safety from a father that was crazy, but to live with a sex offender against court order.

There is also a policeman in this story. His name from the girls is Uncle Ernie. We know of two Ernie's in the police departments. One of those Ernie's came to court to testify in Devil's behalf. Why? My son tells the courts that his daughters are fearful of "Uncle Ernie". He comes over and hurts them at Shorn's house. As time passes their stories become so scary I can barely process and think about them. Uncle Ernie comes over in a cop car, which he backs into the garage. He has on a radio of sorts and he can hear what is happening. There are people at the front door and back door. Men come, three at a time. The children are brought into the living room at Shorns' where they live. Shorn would go one night a week and stay with Floyd before they married. The men would come late a night, three at a time. Layla said she'd watch out the window and three more men would come. And after them three more would come. One time, a man said "How much for those two?" (Layla and Emily are identical twins) And Monster would say "this could be a problem"……..""this might cost a lot more"…….The judge acted as though we were insane. The mother Devil claimed we were crazy. But we weren't crazy. We knew this truth the girls were telling us was horrific and no one was going to help them. It was just horrific in its scope. In this mix of men, and one woman, they tell the children, that if their father doesn't stop talking they will kill him. It is often that the girls tell me "Monster, Monster, says he's going to kill you if you don't shut up." On one trip to see the girls at my son's house, during this time, Devil had orders that the girls could only be seen with her father's presence, because my son took them to the hospital (hospital visits is a story unto itself, later) the girls had to see their father, and our family at Mick's house with TJ present. While we were there TJ fell asleep in the chair.. Layla went into the bathroom at one point. I heard her calling my name. "Mim……Mim will you come in here". My experience since the damn had burst, was that when they called me into a room, it was because they wanted to tell me something. She said "Uncle Ernie was at my house, and he said he's going to kill my daddy? You don't think he'll kill my daddy do you?" I said "Oh honey, I don't think he'll do that. Please don't cry. Why are you saying this." She said Can I say a bad word…..I said "okay"……Because I heard Monster, at my house say to Uncle Ernie, lets kill that son of a bitch. That'll shut him up." And they both started laughing. With that she burst into tears.

People don't realize when they discount our feelings, or the feelings of these little girls, that this is a hell that no one should live in. No grandmother should have to hear this agony from her beautiful little grandchild. No father should have to face this type of hell on his babies….no little girls should ever have to tell such a story. It's hell..

I'd like to ask the "friends" of Monster and Devil……..what if this was happening to you?

As an aside for the few, the ugly, the friends (devils) of Monster and Devil who have put ugly messages on facebook……..ask yourself this.

I went to the police in Bourbonnais when I realized what the girls were saying was happening to them was criminal. After I told my story to the police officer, he said to me "I know what you're telling me is the truth, because I prosecuted Monster when he was convicted for raping his little half sister." I didn't go in and say he robbed banks, he did drugs, (I am told he does), he beat up women, he stole cars.........I said he was molesting little girls. And guess what, I was right. I didn't want to be right, but I was, and I am. Sex offender, is a sex offender, is a sex offender. They are ill in ways that psychiatrists, doctors, nobody understands. It's a horror that cannot be treated, cannot be healed, and is insatiable. That is what we have been told.

After the police report, the girls were taken by Devil in DCFS where they were questioned. We were told by Greg of DCFS that each child had an adult with them.. Devil was with Layla, Shorn was with Emily and TJ was with Annie. Coverage. The room they waited in was miked for the police to hear. Greg and the police officer had to go into the room, and tell them to stop coaching the children. The adults were repeating over and over "Remember Monster didn't hurt you, he'd never yurt you, you're fine, remember he didn't hurt you." The mantra had begun. Greg and Officer Suprenant ran in to the room and said 'You can't coach the children." but they had. The damage had been done. The interview went on from there. They were too afraid to speak, although they said Annie then 3, told them she couldn't tell what Monster does because then her Mommy couldn't marry him. But the damage was done.. The damage is done routinely. Devil, Shorn, and TJ seeing to it that a convicted sex offender has his meat. The children are not allowed to speak the truth. They know this very well.

But Devil's friends believe he's a wonderful guy, and do not protect the children in any way. It is truly insufferable. I ache for the loss of childhood for my granddaughters. I ache to hold them and see them and hug them. I ache for them, knowing that they are facing hell as a daily living.

The mother lied to the courts. Said she feared my son, that he was crazy, that he was delusional. And the courts sided with her, and allowed her to move the children from Illinois to Texas. (Not to live with Monster, however, which is what she did!) She received a two year order of protection, yet again, with no proof of anything. Not one phone call, not one arrest record, not one argument. Just her own lies. She should be a professional liar. Like the old character Jon Lovitz used to do. She'd put him to shame. However, the court appointed, let me repeated, the court appointed psychologist, said that my son was not at all delusional. That every fear and worry he had was well founded, because Monster, Monster was indeed a sex offender. And Monster had called the psychologist, and threatened her. She had requested that she interview him along with everyone else involved in the children's lives. After his threats she requested that her interview with Monster take place at the courthouse, with police presence as he had threatened her!!!! The judge did not allow that. The judge was made known that this Monster had threatened the court appointed expert regarding the safety of the children, and Monster got away with it. Again, lights on, nobody's home.

As Richard Pryor used to say "You came to court expecting someone to listen and care......its just us.....there's no Justice......its just us."

And he's right. The mother Devil lied from day one. Convinced her little girls to lie. They didn't know any better. They're little girls. Whenever she took them for police interviews or for DCFS interviews she'd tell them to lie. The girls told us repeatedly. She actually told them if they told the truth she'd go to jail. Can you imagine going to a psychologist that the father has paid $10,000 for the court review, and telling the children to lie. She cried and said "I'll go to jail." My son went to pick up the girls after they'd been there, and they ran and got the big toys she bought for them because they lied. Emily had a huge teddy bear. They're little girls. They listen to Mommy. Pathetic. Beyond pathetic

How do you fight a Devil and a Monster? It appears you don't. If a mother chooses to make her children sex slaves for her sex offender boyfriend, then that's the way it will be.

And the judge, Shorn, TJ, Floyd, Rocksy, Sorry, Devil and Monster all decided that Monster would have his meat.

On 12/19/08, Devil placed a note on my son Mick's house.

*Mick,*

*Girls and I stopped by to see ya, & they wanted to let you know they want to come tomorrow. I will drop them off around 10:30. If that doesn't work you need to let me know. Get your phone fixed, they miss talking to ya!!*

*Devil, Layla, Emily and Annie*

And a few months later, this lying Devil, gets a two year order of protection that the father cannot see the children for two years. Two years.

Yes there is a Devil.

# Chapter 4 - When the truth is found to be lies

Very shortly after my son and I went to the police and filed a police report regarding the molestation of the girls, after their April 29, 2007 outbursts, we received a letter in the mail from a lawyer.

Devil had gone to her lawyer and drafted a document that stated she had received zero, as in a big fat zero on the piece of paper, from my son, since their divorce. In fact, he had paid her regularly with cash, which I thought was crazy. But we did have many many written receipts from her with her signature.

So many people told us that once she was shown to have lied on a legal document and signed her name to it, she would be known as a liar, and the judge would no longer listen to anything she said. I'd like to tell these people that I can sell them a bridge very cheaply. She has done nothing but lied, and been repeatedly awarded everything they could possibly award her. She is treated as a poor darling woman who is being chased and tortured by her ex husband, which is such an amazing lie. She is a horrendous mother who trafficks her children to a sex offender. And her family and friends tell whatever lie, and manufacture whatever they have to to make this possible for the sex offender.

My son of course was stunned. But we knew the other shoe was to drop. She always had her dirty little tricks book to go back to.

So as we originally went to court to talk about the continual sexual abuse of the children, by a sex offender, it was muddied up by a mother who claimed she was paid zero child support. We did however receive on September 20, 2007 a court order that stated very clearly,

> **1. Devil Mazur shall not reside with the convicted sex offender Monster Thomson. (The Devil had that changed to adjudicated, which actually means plead guilty to.)**

**2. The minor children shall have no contact with Monster Thomson except as authorized by the department of children and family services. (This to me was and is stunning. Why in the world would the department of children and family services ever want the children to have contact with a sex offender.)**

**3. The department of children and family services shall monitor the situation.**

This order was never honored. Ever.

The police would do nothing to protect the children.

I sent a copy of the court order to the police in Manteno, Illinois, as Monster Thomson had sold his condo in Bourbonnais, when the department of children and family services removed the children from his home. I felt the police should know about this order, in order to keep an eye out for the children, and for their safety, and the safety of other children in Manteno. The girls had actually already told us that Monster Thomson has the children over all the time, and other people come over to hurt them.

So I sent a copy to the Manteno Illinois police department. Devil called my son and laughed at him. She found it hysterical. She said "You think the Manteno police department will help you!" He said "We had hopes..." She laughed and told him that she had her connections in the police department and they would help her. Which we found really odd. How can the police department help you, when your boyfriend is a sex offender who is not allowed to be with your children? How can they help you?

So, a friend of ours in downstate Illinois, who was married to a psychiatrist, hired a private detective to look into this. The psychiatrist, Linda, did this entirely unbeknownst to anyone in our family. She later called us very concerned, to tell us what had happened.

It seems that the private investigator had gone to Monster Thomson's apartment to watch what was happening at his apartment. He had his night goggles from his days in Vietnam, his binoculars, and a camera. He sat for a very short time, in the parking lot of Monster's apartment building, just waiting and watching.

Within minutes, police were upon him. They asked him what he was doing. They asked him "Why did Lou send you? What did she tell you?" The officers went about telling him that I was crazy and Monster Thomson was healed. That he couldn't have possibly raped these little girls, as he was healed.

First of all sex offenders of children never heal. Pedophiles are the one oddity in this world, that can never heal. They never stop. And they were law enforcement officers who were knowingly refusing to offer an order from the bench of a judge in their district, who ordered, no contact from this sex offender with these children.

These officers asked the private detective if he'd like to be arrested for drug possession or leave and never come back. Then they threw down a package of cocaine on him. He obviously was very frightened. The police officer again told him, "Lou is crazy. Monster Thomson is healed."

Then two Illinois state police squad cars were called in to escort this man back to Champaign from Manteno. He was told to leave, or he'd be thrown in jail. And who are the criminals?

His goggles, his camera, and his binoculars were taken. The state police escorted him back down I57 to Champaign.

The psychiatrist, Linda, told us that we were in something very big and very serious. She felt by the reaction, and the involvement of the police, that these little girls were part of a sex ring, and we were sniffing in territory that was unsafe. She told us that we had better be very careful, or something bad would happen to us. She felt the girls were being trafficked, and we were way to close for comfort.

This became glaringly apparent with every court date, every movement we had in Kankakee county, and with every contact with the mother.

She had her connections. We did not. She would come into court and be taken to a private area of the courthouse, and brought up in the elevators to the courtroom with police protection, because she had told everyone my son was a dangerous person. Amazing. This woman did not care about anything but trafficking these children to a sex offender. Amazing.

When my son called her in utter shock and had found two large pubic hairs in the baby's diaper (this is how long this has been ongoing) she actually laughed and said "I have pubic hairs in my pants too, you'd better call the cops."

It was all fun and games for her. She could've cared less about her children.

And let me reiterate, at this time, there was a court order that stated that Monster Thomson, sex offender, could have no contact with these children. Why didn't the Manteno police care about that? Why wasn't that their focus? The safety of three little girls. More concerned about the safety of a sex offender, who was ordered to stay away from three little girls!

A court order ignored. Ignored. Special protection for a sex offender.

But these same police officers would come into court and take the stand and lie for the mother to move the children to Texas to live with the Monster.

Horrors. Absolute horrors.

# Chapter 5 - Beautiful Girls

I haven't really taken the time to tell how much I love my granddaughters and what wonderful little girls that they are.

They had wonderful compassion and kindness in them. They were funny, they were sweet, they were great players.

When the twins were about 2 years old, I would go pick them up and keep them for about three or four days. Annie was a baby and Devil had her hands full. So I tried to help as much as I could.

You'd think she would've appreciated this. She didn't. All she ever did was complain about me.

Layla and Emily would play and play. When it was time for a nap, I had two baby cribs in a bedroom upstairs. I would sing to them, and they'd sing along, and I'd stand between the cribs and slide them back and forth a few inches. They'd sing with me until they fell asleep. They'd wake up and be so happy. They'd play their little hearts out. And they'd go down for a nap without one squabble. They did whatever you asked them to do. Good little girls.

We live on a corner across from the junior high school. All the buses for the town would stop there and pick up all the kids and transfer the kids from the other schools to their buses. We'd open the storm door, and they'd watch out the screen door and the windows and watch all the buses coming and the kids loading and unloading. When they'd first see the first bus they'd come running and yell "they're coming, the buses are coming." And they'd watch the twenty minute ritual of all the buses coming together and all the kids getting on their buses.

They would tell me that one day they'd ride the buses and go to school. They absolutely loved it. When they'd get up from their daily naps they'd want to know how soon the buses were coming, and begin their ritual of watching out the window. Silly funny little girls, and we had so much fun.

I'd keep them for three or four days, and take them home and pick up the baby. She was then maybe three months or so old. I'd bring her home, and take care of her for three or four days. She was adorable. I adored that baby.

She slept great. She behaved so well. She was just wonderful. I'd get up with her in the night and feed her and change her, and she'd go right back to sleep.

Devil always propped the bottles with a pillow either lying them down, or with the twins, they would always have a bottle propped in their baby swings. As I recall they basically lived in their swings.

I remember well Mick calling me once and telling me that Devil was angry that I held Annie when she had her bottle. Because Devil didn't like to be bothered with having to hold her, and when she would come home, she wanted to be held while she had her bottle. She'd fuss when Devil propped up her bottle. So sorry Devil that you had to exert such energy. So sorry that you had to be a Mommy. I guess it made it really easy for Monster to move in and swoop up your kids.

They were also my little artists. We have a big round wooden table in our dining room that we've had for forty years. Got it shortly after we married. It has been the sight of much art work and homework with my children and my grandchildren. And many a family dinner. My oldest son is an artist, and I had always had art supplies for my kids. With the girls it was no different. We always had markers, paints, crayons, paper, coloring books, craft paper, construction paper.....I'd clear the table and ask them what they wanted to work on. These little girls would set up shop and begin their art work, and sometimes they'd stay busy for hours. They'd just color and draw and laugh. They'd bring me their pictures to show me their pretty flowers, sunshines, houses, everything that their little hearts thought up. I loved little children's art work because they never worry about what they're drawing or if its right, they just jump into it with abandon. I have many lovely pictures they've drawn, that say "I love you Daddy", or "I love you Mim and Papa"......they were just loving and sweet.

When the girls would all spend the night, sometimes their Daddy worked the night shift (after the divorce) and I would take the girls upstairs to their daddy's room. The twins would lie sideways on the bed, (a queen size bed) I'd be in the middle of them, and Annie would be in her crib next to the bed. I'd put an arm under one twin's neck and reach my hand to Annie and hold her little hand. My other arm would be under the other twin's neck. We'd lie in bed and tell stories or sing, til they fell asleep. It was so funny because Annie would always want to stand up and listen, and I'd keep saying "Lie down baby, you're tired." Finally she'd lie down and hold my hand. It's a sweet memory that brings me to tears. We'd all tell stories about the day and sing, til they fell asleep. Annie was usually first, and I'd know when her little grasp on my fingers would open and her little hand would fall away. Until that time, her little fingers would rub my hand. Emily was usually second, and Layla would stroke and stroke my hand til she fell asleep. When they would all be asleep, I'd lie there and listen to them breathe, and watch their darling little faces. I would sometimes lie there for half an hour just soaking them in. It's a treasure. A definite treasure.

I'll never forget one time I went to pick the girls up for a visit. The twins were coming. I could hear Annie crying and crying in the house. And I mean hollering. Terrible, piercing. I said "something's wrong." Devil assured me she was fine. She was loading the twins into my car. My gut told me something was very wrong. She was still very little. I remember going into the house, and into her room, to piercing cries. When I got in the room, she was on her face, and I mean on her face, nose to the crib, tears pouring out of her eyes, unable to move her face to the side. Still really little. Screaming, terrified. Her hands were down at her sides, and she was kicking her legs as hard as she could. This had been going on at least three to four minutes when I pulled up, so how long had it really been going on? She was hysterical. She was beat red, and could not catch her breath. I picked her up, and she was sobbing. She couldn't calm herself. It took me a good ten minutes to calm her. And she was beside herself. Not crying to be a brat. Crying because she couldn't breathe and was terrified. My son came in and asked me what had happened. I think he had just gotten home. I told him. He took the baby and hugged her and kissed her. I later learned that Devil scorned him terribly for my interference. Interference? How about a baby in a terrible situation. On her face, unable to breathe. Nice mother. I knew of a baby who died when a babysitter put him face down on a bean bag chair. He couldn't breathe. And passed out and died. Devil just frightened the hell out me then, with her lack of concern for her children. And that fright was very well intended, as she has now served up her children to a sex offender. Sex offenders have one thing that they will do until they die. Rape children. And lets get rid of that word molestation forever. When you anally rape a child, when you force your penis upon a child, in their vagina, and in their mouth, and in their anus, you are raping a child. You aren't molesting anything. You are raping a child. And its disgusting. And when people say it has nothing to do with sex. Well, yes it does. If it had nothing to do with sex, then men wouldn't insert their sexual organs into a child's sexual orifice. It's rape. It's cruel, its disgusting.

She never liked that I spent a lot of time with the children. (But she loved not having to deal with them.) She felt they should be on their own. But at my house, we had a blast. We painted, we drew pictures, we read books, we made pizzas, we watched funny movies, we played outside, we went for walks, we went to the park, we rode bikes, with training wheels for quite awhile, we had fun. That fun and that time are now treasures to me. I draw upon them when I miss the girls, which is every moment of my life. To take them from us, and place them with a sex offender against court order, is just a huge knife in the back. And for the girls, it is hell. I know it is hell. I still can't believe that no one listened or cared about three little girls.

I loved when we would decorate the Christmas tree. I loved it so much. They would get the decorations and put them all low on the tree, cause they were little. It was darling. After they'd go home, I'd straighten them out a bit, but they got pretty darn good at decorating the lower part of the tree for me. I even let them decide at times where to put other decorations. I am a Christmas freak. I love it. I love it. I decorate every inch of my house, and I live in a hundred year old house that has the beautiful woodwork, and a large staircase, and all the makings of a beautiful Christmas. And they were always the biggest part of that holiday.

Every year we would take a picture for the Christmas card. I'll never forget the year that we got them beautiful long little satin Christmas dresses that had a long tie in the back, with silk blouses and beautiful little shoes. Ruffly little socks, and they had their hair done in long beautiful curls. They were so beautiful. They all looked like little China dolls. They stood in front of the tree long enough for the picture to be snapped, and then they'd run to the photographer so they could see the picture. They loved being beautiful, and being told they were beautiful. And God they were beautiful. Every picture I have of them they are beautiful, smiling, happy, in some they are beaming. And there's a vibrance in their eyes and their being. The pictures I have seen of them since their mother Devil took them away, they look sad. Their hair is chopped off, and not even brushed, (if you tell I'll cut off all your hair), they aren't smiling, they aren't happy. It's sad. No little girl should be unhappy with a Monster. No mother should allow it.

They were the best little pizza makers in the world. I loved Chicago deep dish pizza. So I found a pizza cooker and a recipe book on the internet and bought it. They would help me make the dough, and knead the dough. They loved helping in the kitchen. I didn't have to ask for help. I'd say "I'm going to start the pizza dough, anyone want to".............before I could finish my thought all three girls would be running into the kitchen and Annie would have gotten the little wooden booster chair to get up to the table to help. They'd mix it and stir it and then they'd divide it up in three pieces and knead the dough. I have many pictures of this, and many memories. After the dough would rise, they would make the pizza. And yes they made the pizza. I'd give them the sauce and all the ingredients, and tell them what was next, and they'd make a gorgeous pizza. When it was done, (they'd often go to the "dinger" or the timer and watch it to see if it was almost done. They'd sit in front of their pizza, and everyone would come to the table. They were so proud. So proud of what they had done. They would sit so they were all as close to the pizza as they could and wait for compliments. They'd get many. They were just the most wonderful little girls in the world. Telling you how much I miss them and how I anguish over their circumstances is so real and so horrific to me......its hard to take it all in. Hard to understand. Hard to believe. This is happening in America in the year 2011.

We would tell dream stories, and they'd tell me all the things they wanted to do someday. We'd talk of our "favorites"......favorite food, favorite tv show, favorite person, favorite story, favorite time, favorite day....sometimes it would get so funny and we'd laugh and laugh. I just adored any time with them. I'm sure everyone loves their grandchildren, and can relate to what I am saying. Being with them, enjoying them, loving them, caring for them, being part of their lives was a treasure. I treasure every moment I had with those little ones. I have that in my heart, and in my memory forever.

I believe I could go on, and forever treasure them, but the horrors they face, tear at my soul, and my conscience. I can't come to terms with what is happening to them. And I definitely cannot come to terms with no one caring that this is happening to them. It just burns my core. Burns my heart. When all of this first came to light, I could barely handle it.

I would have a picture of them that I kept very close, so I could pick it up and look at them. I'd stare at their little faces, and tell them how very sorry I was that no one helped them, that they were in this situation, and pray that one day they would know how very hard we tried to save them. For three long years we fought for their safety and their rights. No one cared and no one listened. How do you tell that to a little girl?

The judge had written in one of her orders that we could not talk to the children about the other parents. The children told us all the time that their mother was taking them to the sex offender.

54

They wanted to know what the stuff was that came out of Monster's bat....the white stuff. Why was Mommy letting him do that? Why doesn't Mommy make him stop. The children had even said that they'd like Daddy to kill Monster, please kill Monster so that it would stop.

Again, we felt like we had landed in hell. We were trying to give these little girls a childhood. Safety, fun, cooking, laughing, playing. With Mommy, sex abuse, sex offender, rape, torture.

I just can't begin to tell you how deep and horrific the pain has been for me and my family! And its not even happening to us. It's happening to little girls. Little girls. They are now 9 and 8, and this hell is still going on. Unfathomable.

# Chapter 6 - The Emperor Has no Clothes

My sisters' husband, John knew a state representative. He had worked previously on some local council with her. He felt he knew her well enough to contact her and ask for help.

John called this woman, I'll call Lisa. He asked her to please help us, as the girls were suffering terribly, and no one would step up and help them. Lisa directed John, for us to take the girls to the hospital and have them examined. Once we had proof of the injuries, she would step in and help the children get to safety.

So, my sister Diana, my son Mick, and I decided to take Layla and Emily first.. Two children would be enough to take care of, and we would take Annie later.

We called the hospital in Kankakee, (we had been told we needed a critical care unit that had the proper equipment), and the nurse spoke with the doctor. The doctor very kindly said "bring them now.." I said they really needed to get dressed and eat something.. The nurse said "bring them as they are, we will feed them something here."

When we got to the hospital the doctor couldn't have been nicer or more accommodating. He wanted us and the girls to be comfortable. He wanted to know the words that the girls used for private parts, and any words they might say that he was not familiar with. My son told him they called their vagina, a chachi, and they called a man's penis, a bat.

DCFS was called. Also KC Casa which was another child's agency for child welfare was called. Their representatives would come later.

The doctor was ready to examine the children. I went in with Emily. I said nothing, as I realized they wanted to hear her speak. The doctor placed an instrument in her vagina that was a camera that could see the damages if any. There was a television type screen over the bed. The doctor looked at the nurse, and pointed to the television. They both gave each other knowing looks. It was a torn posterior fourchetta couchette I later learned. This happens two ways. Childbirth, and rape. I know this five year old girl had never experienced childbirth.

The doctor asked Emily if anyone touched her there, or if anyone hurt her there. Emily replied "Monster puts his bat in my chachi. And he puts his hands in my chachi." Emily also said 'He made me watch while Monster played with himself and Layla."

Layla said in her interview "Monster played with himself and touched my chachi with his penis." Emily also stated "Monster is touching me in my private parts down there in front and in my chachi." Points to her vaginal area. She has yellow discharge from vagina. She said it happened " between Halloween and Thanksgiving at her gramma's house. "

The doctor teared up after he examined Emily. I was not in the room with Layla and I never really asked what happened, as I had seen enough to make me ill with Emily. Layla went into the room with her Daddy. These poor little girls. Poor little girls.

The doctor turned around after Emily's exam and reached into his pocket, and wiped away his tears. He handed Emily a five dollar bill and told her she was a sweet little girl, and she should get herself and her sister an ice cream cone.

The DCFS and KC Casa workers were then at the hospital. They wrote up paperwork to have the children taken from their mother for two weeks for a safety plan. They were to have no contact with Monster nor Devil for two weeks, while the children had follow up treatment for their injuries, and were able to speak with a therapist to find out the extent of what was happening to them.

The DCFS worker had to call his office and have a supervisor sign off on the paperwork. Which was done.

We left the hospital after several hours, feeling that the girls might be safe, finally. We stopped at the police station in Kankakee to show them the paperwork, and tell them the children would be in Watseka at our home.

The police understood, and wished us well.

That night we went home, and felt like we had actually achieved something. We felt the girls might be safe. Emily was thrilled. She realized that finally someone would help her. We were to go for follow up treatment the next day, and get some help for her injuries. Layla was also to be examined by her own doctor. At the emergency room their injuries had merely been documented. They were to have follow up.

The next day, early morning I called their doctor, who happened to be in Kankakee. I felt with the safety plan, and the orders of the agencies, we would be safe.

We got ready to go. It was early December so it was cold. My son gave me his phone, and the girls and I got ready to go. Emily was just ecstatic. Layla was happy too. Finally, someone would listen. Someone would care. Emily would have treatment and it hurt badly. She kept telling me on the way there, "I'm getting help. It hurts Mim, and he's going to help me."

We got to Kankakee in about forty minutes. We went into the doctor's office. Dr. Oo. We were taken into the doctor's offices fairly quickly. The girls were told to strip and put on gowns. Then we waited and waited and waited and waited. I had told the nurse at the desk, that this was a criminal investigation, and these girls had rape injuries. I said "If the mother should call, don't tell her anything."

While I was gone, my son had received a phone call. From Detective Etzel. He and Claire Tiffany of DCFS wanted the children returned immediately to the mother. What? Yes, he wanted the children returned immediately. If we did not, my son would be arrested. We had one hour.

They asked my son where the children were. He told them that I had taken them to the doctor. So, the mother and the police were on their way to pick up the children!

I had a nurse come into the room and tell me to answer the phone. I went out and Mick was on the phone. He was hysterical. "Get out of there, she's coming. She's coming with the police." I couldn't comprehend. What? We have a two week safety plan in which she is suspect, and is to be investigated. No. Not happening.

I ran into the room, and said to the girls "get dressed, we have to leave.."

In that moment the nurse knocked on the door.

"The mother and the police want to speak with you."

I was frozen in time. I felt like I was waiting to be swallowed by a hungry lion. I couldn't move. I couldn't think.

I said "What did you just say?"

She said "The mother is here to take her children, with the police."

I walked to the outer office with my paperwork. I tried to speak. The police officer barreled past me with the mother and said "We need no paperwork, we're taking the kids."

I was dumbfounded. In shock. Just complete shock. I ran back to the room to get my coat and keys. I couldn't speak. I just turned and ran. I felt devastated. Little did I know the power of a mother who served up her kids to a sex offender. Dumb. I was dumb. Who is pulling these strings?

I went to the state representative's office to talk to her. I pulled on the door, and it was locked. And there was no place to leave any information. So I ran back to the Explorer to leave. The truck wouldn't start! I called my son to tell him what happened. He said that he tried to call me, but his phone that he had given me, was on vibrate, not ring. So I wasn't aware of it.

I called my Mom, who came to help me. She lives in Kankakee. She came to get me, and we called a tow truck. We went to her house, and waited for a phone call. He finally came and started the truck. I ran and got gas, and ran to my sister's to drop off the paperwork for the state representative, who was to help us.

I ran to my oldest son's house to pee, as I hadn't peed for hours. I was spent, I was dead.

I had thrown the phone down when I called home, while the truck was dead, only to be told the police were there to pick up Annie. With no paperwork. I felt broken. I felt dead. I wondered where God was. Did he know all of this was happening to little girls? What had they ever done to deserve a mother that allowed them to be raped. I really felt like I'd fallen into the pits of hell. I didn't know how to breathe. I didn't know where to turn. I felt like someone had pulled my brain and my heart out of me and jumped on them. I was walking wounded. If I felt this badly, what did our little girls feel?

Every time I would have a clairvoyant moment, trying to make sense trying to understand, trying to figure out which foot went in front of the other, I would think of the pain the girls were living through, and I would fall apart.. Who assists a sex offender? Who ignores the report of a physician in an emergency room, and delivers the girls back to the predators? Who does that?

And the physician who examined the girls, was the head physician of that emergency room for 25 years. I think he was very aware of what had happened to them.

Falling apart seemed all I could do. I knew Mick was falling apart. I to this day, do not know how he has weathered the hell that Devil has placed upon his children. What mother in this world could possibly do something so horrific to her own children? It is something I will never be able to wrap my brain around. Never. Never.

Her vicious nature has no bounds. One day when she had kept the children from Mick for three months, he finally reached her at her father's house. The children were there and he wanted to talk to them. She said to him "You mean you haven't killed yourself yet?" This gave me great pause for a number of reasons.. Who would ever suggest to another human being, who is the father of her children, that he should go kill himself, and be upset that he hasn't yet killed himself? And it also gives me great pause, as I am well aware, that her first affair, while she was married to my son, was to a young man, who was a good friend to my son. We'll call him Jerry. And Jerry in fact took his own life after their affair was ended. What a mean evil creature this monster is. Evil.

Devil. Devil. Devil. She is a pure creation of hell.

I would like to add, that Devil also lied in filing a complaint with the courts when my son and she split up. She did nothing but lie. But the lie that really has hurt my son, in his job, and in his life, was that he battered her.

He never laid a hand on her. He had gone to her house, (her mother's house) to show Devil a table he bought for the girls for his new house. She was going to Mick's house all the time to be with him, and leaving the children with him all the time. To the point that the police came to his house to present him with a new protective order against her and the children, while the children were with him. The officer was stunned. Mick told him "she lies all the time." But no one ever stopped her. And the judge kept handing her these ridiculous pieces of paper. Like I said before, like buying gum.

Anyway, Mick had gone to her mother's house to show her the table, as he was fixing it up for the girls, and had told her about it. He was simply stopping by her Mom's to show it to her.

As he approached the house from the back, he saw through the basement window where Devil had her family room. Indeed in the basement on the couch, embraced lovingly, was Devil and Jerry. Mick's mind exploded. She had tooled him yet again. She had made him believe they were going to work things out. That they would be a family again.

When in fact, she had started going to school at night to be a phlebotomist. However, at the class breaks she would meet Jerry, and go into his car and perform oral sex on him. This is what Jerry told Mick. Jerry finally could no longer take the lies and pain he felt in this mess. So he told Mick the story of their affair. Devil had started a relationship with him, and was having sex with him on a regular basis. And all the while coming to Mick's house and having a relationship with him. Devil.

So when Mick saw them in the basement, before he was aware of everything that was going on, he simply lost it. So much had happened. So much.

And here she was. With this man. The man she had brought to his house to play cards, all the while playing footsie with him under the table. The man she had at the house the night that Mick moved out. Mick had gone back later that night just to see if anything was happening. Indeed as he approached the house, he saw a neatly cleaned living room, with a gift on the table. Perfume that Jerry had bought for Devil.

And he walked around to the bedroom, outside, and could hear that they were indeed having sex. He came into the house and confronted them.

So when he saw him in her basement, yet again, and realized all the lies that both of them were filling him with, he became enraged. Wrong, yes. He knocked on the door. When Devil came to the door, he pushed her backwards and went after Jerry. He indeed beat him up. Which was wrong. But I believe that this is how males react. Sometimes with their fists.

The police came. Mick was arrested. Devil filed charges of domestic battery. He never laid a hand on her.

He did push her out of the way, which was wrong.

He had to go to court several times to fight that charge. He was working in Chicago at the time. So he'd have to leave work repeatedly to go to court. Devil and Shorn both actually came to court to try to get the charges dropped. For what reason Devil actually had a moment of clarity and honesty I don't know. But Mick's lawyer, at that time, who is actually a distant relation. told him to just go ahead and plead guilty and get it over with. The d.a. said she wouldn't drop the charges. Faced with more court dates, and driving back and forth repeatedly, he stupidly plead guilty. He thought getting it over with at the time was the best thing. He wanted it over, and to move forward.

This has been something that has harmed him greatly. It comes up all the time in background checks for a job. It's a nightmare. But then again, what more could we expect. Just more of the same.

Jerry's dead. Mick's destroyed. The children are part of a sex ring. Devil's family lies to keep the children in danger. And Devil and Monster are happy.

And all of this happened well before Monster Thomson came onto the scene. I believe this was within the first four months after they separated. We are now into five plus years of this hell going on.

The "battery" was against Jerry. Had nothing to do with Monster. Devil merely used this to her advantage to repeatedly get bogus orders of protection.

I would also like to add, that Devil's supposed "upset" about this is a tad derelict. Her own brother Mark, found his wife in bed with another man, and beat the hell out of him. And he sees his children.

And Devil's family did not have a problem with this. They thought she deserved it. She didn't. But it shows how people's minds change when its someone they are related to.

# Chapter 7 - Burning Down the House

As God is my witness, I do not know exactly when or how I learned all of the horrors my granddaughters told us about. I have tried to block much of what they've said as its too horrific to listen to or take into my conscious. Because once I acknowledge that I have heard it, and understand it, I have to acknowledge to myself that my granddaughters, these tiny little girls, that I adore, that I love, are being sexually assaulted. Repeatedly.

And sadly the horrors go further. The girls tell us that they have to go to Monster's apartment, and stay with him. They tell Mommy Devil that they don't want to, and she says "He loves you, you'll have fun." Then she leaves. Then several men, and one woman, show up, and hurt them. They are made to strip and have things put inside them. They toy with the children, and pull on their clothing, and laugh, and strip them, and hurt them. They tell me that Annie is bashful and doesn't like to be naked. I bow my head in anguish and horror, as I realize that no one cares, and no one will help them.

They tell me that these men take out their bats and put them in their chachis, in their butts, in their mouths, til the stuff comes out, and it hurts. My blood drains from my body at the thought of this hell. It's truly more than I can bear. To think that these darling little girls, that are my loves, my babies, my granddaughters, are sexual slaves to all these horrific monsters is something I can barely think of. Barely entertain in my mind. Horrific. What kind of a mother Devil allows this to happen?

A judge told you in court that Monster could have no contact with these children, and you leave them alone with him. Any mother worth her salt would protect her children. It is so disgusting and repulsive.

God help us. God help us. I fear that something must be done before these little girls are killed. Grown men can't have sex with little tiny girls and not have something horrific happen. And grown men on drugs. We have been told that Monster does cocaine. Grown men on cocaine having sex with little girls. Could anything in this world be more disgusting? I have watched horror moves and war movies where foul disgusting men rape little children, and it is horrific. This bastard has the mother's blessing to rape her little girls. She serves them up to him. For his pleasure.

While I hope he dies in jail, I believe that the mother is far more vile and reprehensible than he. She allows it. She has been told by the courts that he is a child molester , that the children cannot be with him, and she serves them up. And she lies about him being with the children. And her family, including Shorn, her mother, and Floyd, her mother's boyfriend, and all of her family and friends, lie so that Monster can have access to the children. Have I died and gone to hell?

What on this earth could be more foul?

As a very strange aside, why did the police in Manteno harass a private detective who was watching a sex offender, who was court ordered not to be with these three little girls? If he is healed, then why are they roughing up the private detective? If the children aren't there, why are the police so overreacting? Why in the world are the police on the side of a sex offender? The Devil proudly called my son to tell him, that she had friends in the Manteno police department, and they would do what she wished. She wished for her children to be raped? I had sent the court order that Monster could have no contact with the children, as I knew he lived in Manteno, and I wanted them to keep an eye out for the safety of my granddaughters. The police actually harassed and threatened to arrest a private detective who went to Manteno, unbeknownst to us, to watch Monster. As soon as he parked his vehicle the police arrived and questioned him as to what he was doing there. They asked him, had I sent him to spy on Monster? They let him know that I was crazy, and Monster was healed. Healed? Hmmm. Why are the Manteno police not honoring a court order in their county, and why are they defending a sex offender? Unbelievable! No one in the police department, the states attorney's offices, nor the judges made any sense in this case. They all were beholding to

66

Devil and Monster. There is no concern for the safety of three little girls against a big monster.

My brain cannot take it all in. Very difficult. Little tiny girls that no one will help. I know that these people go to church, have families, know right from wrong, take some sort of oath.......why won't they protect my granddaughters?

On one occasion when Annie was at our home, she came into the kitchen and showed me her tummy. Across her chest and tummy, someone had taken a razor blade and etched some type of devil worshiping signs into her flesh. Ever so slightly so it would heal. I said "Honey what happened.' She said "Monster took a blade and cut me." On another occasion Annie found a circular small blade that my son used at work. She brought it into the kitchen and held it to her throat, and said "This is what Monster does to us.' And she pulled the razor across her neck, as if someone was slashing her throat, and made a creepy sound. Remember we cannot take the children to the doctor!

Thinking about the many times the girls have told us horror stories floods my mind. But no one cares. No one listens. Just thinking about their revelations makes my skin crawl. It is so beyond horrific that they have to endure this hell.

Once Layla came into the house to see me upon arrival for her visitation. She brought in a little notebook. I was at the computer table. She hurried to my side and told me she had to tell me something. She threw her little notebook open and began to draw pictures of little girls being thrown to the floor, by a big man who had a dark face, and told me that Monster is hurting her, and putting things in her chachi, and it hurts.......I gathered myself and said "Why are you telling me this right now, as soon as you walk in the door?" She looked at me, and with a tear welling in her eye said "Because we really need help."

About six weeks after the judge drafted an order of protection against Monster regarding the girls, we had quite an eye opener. We actually believed he was gone. Devil's family had told us that he was gone. He had moved away. He was going to be a professional golfer in Florida. While I found that far reaching, (I'm going to be a professional tennis player!) I was happy he was gone. And Devil's father TJ assured me that it was true. Imagine my shock when my son went to pick up the girls for visitation. He picked up the girls at a nearby grocery store from Shorn's house. This was because Devil had her order of protection because she feared my son, right? As Mick was driving back to leave town after picking up the girls, he looked left down Devil's street where her Mother lived. And low and behold there was Monster. Monster was waiting for Devil to return.

Mick was shocked. He turned to drive by her house. When he was at her house, Devil and Monster came up to his car. Devil and Monster were kicking and hitting the car, and telling him to get the girls out of the car. The girls were screaming, crying, hysterical. Mick drove away and headed to our house. The girls told Daddy that Monster never left. Devil, Shorn, TJ and Monster made it up. The girls were not to tell Daddy. Monster in fact, had never left. Never. The girls were crying, screaming, and hysterical. Devil Mommy was still serving them up. He was still molesting them. (Raping them.) He was babysitting them while Devil worked. (I believe she may have worked one whole year in her life.) He was alone with them. Her family didn't care. He was alone with them. They were sacrificing the girls. Serving them up.

The girls would cry because no one would believe them. Layla told us that at school she got out of line to tell her teacher, and the teacher told her to bet back in line. So much for kindergarten. Most kids are wondering about their pony tails, going out to recess to run, picking new friends: Layla is trying to get out of line and tell someone that she's being sexually assaulted.

At the court date, I will never forget Devil's mother sitting in her seat in the courtroom.

She looks like a pissed off, ragged out, ugly old skank. She was sitting in her pew, shaking her head no while his sexual assault record was being talked about. She sat and shook her head back and forth, no, no, no, while it was being discussed. Doesn't get it. When the order was written and handed down, that he was indeed a sex offender, and should have no contact with the children, she was shaking her head, yes, yes, yes, while the judge spoke. Like a damn bobble head doll. Devil was saying to her lawyer, "but we can call DCFS so he can be with them if we want to go somewhere." What a fabulous idea. Let's fire up the car, make plans, and head out with the kids for a fun day with a sex offender! Not a suspected child molester, but a proven sex offender. A sex offender who is ordered to have no contact!" Devil and her lawyer, that Monster eventually murdered, actually asked the judge to change the word "convicted" sex offender, to "adjudicated" sex offender. I just loved that one. Convicted means that a judge or a jury found you guilty. Adjudicated means that you believe you are guilty. It's true. Your babies are with a found to be true sex offender! Now let's fire up the car and go see the sex offender. Bring the kids! Excuse me but I think I need someone to kiss me. I like to be kissed when I'm being screwed!

My son and I left the courthouse in complete shock. We had kept the girls at our house after they told us Monster was with devil babysitting them stripping them, raping them, putting his penis in their mouths.......on and on and on.....We had called DCFS on Friday night, after the girls freaked out.

The investigator from DCFS came on Saturday. She was from Danville, our district. The girls told her a litany of disgusting situations that they are placed in by the sex offender. Keep in mind he is not even supposed to be with them. He is alone with them, raping them. This investigator talked to the children for at least two hours. She told us that in her experience Monster would be in jail before night fall with two felonies on each child. She sent her report to Kankakee DCFS.

Kankakee DCFS Bob Leonard put her report in the file. We were to return the children immediately. He told us that Monster Thomson sex offender was a healed man. Excuse me? When did that happen. First of all, sex offenders don't heal. And secondly, when was the Monster evaluated? And there is an existing court order that Mr. Thomson, sex offender, Monster, could have no contact with the children! Or was Mr. Leonard doing favors for someone?

I have nothing but disdain and horror in my gut for the system. The DCFS bastards that have done nothing to help these little girls. DCFS decided they liked the mother Devil better than us, because my husband was upset. My husband and I were going to a funeral home the evening that the DCFS man came to speak with us. He told the man "someone needs to help these little girls, and soon before he kills one of them." And with that he informed the man we needed to get to the funeral home, for him to visit his beloved aunt who had passed away. We had spoken at length and we needed to go to the funeral home. This was a beloved aunt who would die all over again if she knew what was happening to these little girls. Thankfully she never knew. She died of natural causes. DCFS decided that my husband's demeanor wasn't what they felt was appropriate, they liked the Devil Mother's demeanor better. All she had to do was act, and she did so very badly, but they liked her, and they believed her. Even when all truth and circumstance showed her as a liar, they stayed with the mother as the person who should have the power over the children. So that her sex offender boyfriend could have access to them!

Emily tells us one day when she comes for visitation, that she had a very bad day. I asked her what was wrong. Her eyes welled with tears. She began by telling me that Monster had come over before school and put his bat in her butt, and it really hurt. She said that it got stuck in her butt, and it wouldn't come out. Monster hit her and pushed on her and said bad words til it came out. She said that her butt was bleeding. She had to go into the bathroom, and put Kleenex in her panties and hope that she would stop bleeding. During school that day she asked to go to the bathroom several times so she could check and see if there was any blood on her clothes. She didn't want anyone to know that Monster had put his bat in her butt. And after school she was so happy that the day had ended so she could go home, and change her clothes. But no one came to school to pick her up. So she had to sit in the office, wondering about the blood in her pants, and if someone would see it. Her Devil Mommy finally came to pick her up.

Oddly enough, a man stopped by our house one day to stop and talk to my husband. My husband is a bike collector. This gentleman is too a collector of trains, and dabbles in bikes. He stopped to talk to my husband about an auction. The girls at that time were running around the yard and playing. He told my husband that they were indeed beautiful little girls. They talked for some time. After the man had said many kind things about the girls being sweet and cute, my husband told him that we have a great sadness regarding the girls. That their mother was indeed involved with a sex offender, and allowed him access to the children all the time.......The man was appalled. He was so very saddened that these darling little girls were being harmed. He offered to help us. We have contacted so many police who have done nothing, state representative who did nothing, judge who could care less, DCFS in Kankakee who did absolutely nothing to help, ....so we felt maybe he would know someone who would help. He took the information to the state policeman that he knew and respected. My son later contacted the state police to tell them all the things that the girls had said was happening to them, and what they had said about Martha D.

The state police did nothing. In fact, the state police helped the mother move the children out of state, to Texas, where they were on a lease with the sex offender, against court orders. If anyone in their right mind expects me to believe that is kosher, I have a bridge I'd like to sell. The police, the courts, the FBI, DCFS, never figured out, or asked where she was moving or asked to see her lease. She was on a lease with THE SEX OFFENDER, MONSTER AND THE CHILDREN. Have I died and gone to hell? Yes. Devil and Monster signed this lease before the final court date. She stated to Monster on April 25, 2009, "I love you baby. It is almost done." It is stripping the father of his parental rights and trafficking the children from Illinois to Texas. The children were also trafficked to Florida, Texas, Oklahoma, Hawaii, and Brazil. And yet the authorities have done nothing.

No one cares that three little girls are being raped by a sex offender and his God awful friends, creatures from hell.

It seems to me that our society should be able to protect the least of these. The young, the old, and the infirm. If you can't do that, then you are destined for hell. I pray that they survive. I pray that they know that we love them, and want a better life for them. I pray that they understand that their Devil Mother and Monster are the scum of the earth. But they are merely little girls.

# My Sweet Little Girls

I Believe in You
Though I have no idea what to do
Or where to turn
I have begged, I have pleaded
No one seems to care
I stop. I pray.
I pray for a day.
When A Devil will know
And will be made to know
That the Monster that she has chosen to love
(How can she even know what love is)
Is in fact tearing your world apart
Maybe she already knows
Obviously does not care
The pain, the fear, the horror that
Has become your life
Three beautiful angels
Handed to the Monster
By their own Mother Devil,
Their very own birth mother,
The revulsion I feel is abhorrent and quick
I can barely comprehend
I pray, I pray.
I stop. I pray.
My mind is burned, my thoughts are twisted,
I pray for little girls who
For nothing they have ever done
Are deemed to be with a Monster sex abuser
And a Devil Mother
Or as little Annie says
Scary Mommy

# Scary Mommy

And yet this SCARY MOMMY
Has fits if
Someone questions the fact
That her own mother was once raped
How could someone not believe
Not believe her mother was raped
As she is the Devil
that doesn't believe her own daughters
Does Not support her own daughters who are raped
Does Not support her own daughters who are raped
Devil and Shorn hated those who didn't believe
The pain supposedly inflicted upon Shorn
When Shorn was supposedly raped
Shorn claimed rape
But how can anyone believe that was her fate
When Shorn refuses to stop a child rapist
Of her own granddaughters
No pain or sadness for her tiny little granddaughters
The babies God gave to us to love and protect
Love and protect
Her own little grandbabies, aged 3 and 5
Who have been raped
Repeatedly raped
Raped
Raped
Raped
As they have told all of us in their little girl words
And they have received no help from anyone
Dismal
Sadistic
Horrific
Shameful
Shameful
Shameful

May God make those who did not believe, and who did nothing to stop your hell, pay for the pain they have allowed to be inflicted upon three beautiful little girls

One of my worst incidents of horror came one evening in January 2008. Little Annie got up in the middle of the night to pee, as she was afraid she'd wet the bed. She was so tired, but happy she'd gotten to the bathroom. After she peed, I asked her if she'd like a diaper for the rest of the night. She would awaken wet, and be so upset......so we decided to put on a pull up. She laid down on the couch. She spread her legs apart for me to put on the pull up. The inside of her vagina was red and swollen. I said 'Oh honey, does this hurt, it looks so sore.' Annie rubbed her eyes, and said "Monster still hurts my chachi, and he burned down that lady's house." I thought she'd had a bad dream or something and I asked her "What did you say?" She repeated "Monster (Monster) burned down Marfa's house. And he has her jewelry." The next day I asked the twins what in the world that meant. They froze over like statues. A few days later when we were in the car alone, they asked me if I wanted to know what happened at Martha's.

As the girls told me, they were taken out of bed one night and taken to a house in the country. It was dark and scary. They had to have big sticks that Monster caught on fire. Emily held hers too close to her clothing and her shirt caught on fire. Monster made her take it off and thrown it down. They then went into the house, and unplugged the phones. They went into the bedroom and the woman cried out "Please don't hurt me." Whereupon she was set on fire. The entire house went up in flames. The girls were told the infamous line "This is what happens to people who f(*k with Monster. Got it?"

The next morning these little girls were going to a follow up interview with DCFS in Chicago. A follow up to our hospital visit, when they told Dr. Kruzak that Monster puts his bat in their chachis.) Does anyone wonder if these little girls had anything to say? I don't. They have been terrorized, raped, scared, into silence. Beyond the raping, they greatly fear what happened to Martha will happen to them. And Monster has told them repeatedly he will kill their Daddy and their Mim if we don't shut up.

Several months later the girls, still in Illinois, before the Devil hijacked them to Monster, the girls and I were near Martha's home. Emily said "Mim, isn't this by Martha's house." Oddly I had lived in that area many years, and knew exactly where she lived. We turned and headed to Martha's house. The site is on a hill. I pulled the car into the driveway. All of my car doors were thrown open and Layla, Emily and Annie ran up the hill. Like being tossed into a familiar environment, they went into a narrative of that night. They showed me where the house door was, where Emily took off her shirt, where they got the sticks that they caught on fire…..they ran the property and babbled for at least ten minutes. Then one of them got very spooked, and said "Let's get out of here." We went back to the car. As we drove away, there was silence. And Emily had a tear in her eye. This is a memory and a hell that no little girls should face. My son told this story to the state police. Their response to him. 'You have a shirt, you think we can do anything with that." The girls also told us that they took all of Martha's jewelry. Monster had her jewelry.

I am in shock as I write this. These memories are burned into my brain. They go on and on. Think of the Martha night from hell. Think of the fear. Think of the anguish of three little girls. Remember *Reservoir Dogs*.....Michael Madsen setting the man on fire.......Monster set this woman on fire.....after breaking into her house, and making little girls watch. Absolute terror. Absolute horror. And I as a grandmother have to live with these thoughts and know that these girls are suffering.

One of my saddest memories was asking the girls to please illustrate a story they told to the DCFS woman from Danville. The girls had told her that Monster puts his bat in their mouths til they choke. I can't believe I didn't understand that, but I had never heard anything like that. I even told it to a police officer, that I later learned had a brother who molested his children. The police officer told me it didn't make any sense. The three girls were on the porch. Late summer night. Beautiful outside. That mood seemed so transposed with what was going on. Beautiful weather, ugly reality. I said "girls, can you explain to me what that means, the bat and the choking. I don't understand." Layla starts to explain to me. "Monster takes his bat, and we all lie down side by side." Like a mime troupe, the other girls began to act it out. Emily lies down on the porch floor and lays perfectly still. Layla continues, "We all lie down on the floor by each other, and Monster goes back and forth like this"….and then she bends her knees and grabs something imaginary at her crotch level…"and Monster grabs his bat, and goes back, and forth and puts his bat in our mouths" …..at that point Annie who is 3, walks toward me and puts her mouth in the shape on an oval…'and then the stuff comes out and we choke"….and with that she puts her arms to her neck and chokes. Little girls, 5 and 3, describing a blow job being performed on them by a child rapist. I began to cry, but very quietly, and tried to maintain my composure, as I was so proud of them for telling me. Layla came over to me and said "It's alright Mim, we're alright." My great sadness had to take a back seat to their strength. Their strength. I do not know the extent of the pain they are suffering, or how often it is happening to them. I do know that it is far too much and it is killing them. I think to myself of grown women enduring rape once, and what it does to them emotionally and I almost fall apart. These little girls are trying like hell for someone, anyone to listen, and no one will. These little girls are suffering.

They are alone in a world of hurt, orchestrated by their very own birth mother, Devil.

I often wonder if Monster and Devil will ever pay for any of the horrors that they have done to these children, and to Martha. Murder is such a strong horror. The taking of a life. And raping little girls. What kind of monster lives inside that creature? Horrific. It is something I can barely think about, and my granddaughters have to live within their hell. The hell created by Devil and Monster.

No one is concerned. No one is lying awake at night and wondering if these children are alive. If they are alright. If they are scared. If the Monster is coming into their room, and hurting them.

They have told us about jail. They hide in the basement and then the Monster comes after them, and catches them, and then they are with the jailer and he hurts them. I hear this and I flinch. I begin to cry, and I have to stop, or I will melt under the pain. The horror of their pain. I can't even think of it. It terrifies me. At the time, I'm 55, and the girls are 5 and 3.

The Monster dresses up like a woman, with his wig, and his makeup and comes after them, and they have to put his bat in their mouth.

God help us. God help us all. I fear that we must have something done before one of these little girls is killed. Grown men can't have sex with little tiny girls and not have something horrific happen, beyond the obvious. Torn little bodies. Pain. Unbearable sadness for these little girls. Could anything be more horrific? These dirty nasty foul men having sex with children because they can. This bastard prostituting these little girls. While I hope he dies a horrible evil death one day at the hands of a father whose child was raped by a sex offender, I also hope a horrific death for Devil. All she had to do was remove the children from the Monster. She spent four years in court lying and destroying the lives of the girls, and of my son, their father, all for a sex offender to have his meat. To provide her children to a sex offender against court orders. To take the children across state lines, and out of the country during a time when they were court ordered to have NO CONTACT with the monster. She served them up. Served them up. For his pleasure.

What could possibly be more foul?

And let me make one thing very clear. He is not a child molester. I hate that word. Molest. Molester. Sounds like someone ruffled up a shirt and wrinkled it. No he is a rapist. A child rapist. He rapes children.

The courts, the police, the state representative, DCFS, everyone we have spoken with says "molester"......no he's a child rapist. But they do nothing to stop him.

And as a child rapist, the horrors become greater and more severe. The Monster is putting some sort of a hook in them, and they bleed. The Monster is putting his penis in their chachis and their butts, and it hurts. And they bleed. Mommy throws away their bloody underwear. Emily says his bat gets stuck in her butt and makes her bleed. I wonder how much more they can take. The private detective that tells me the more they tell, the less he believes. The more they tell, the more I believe. Molesters continue to molest. Rapists continue to rape. Until they are caught. I feel as though we have landed in the land of Dumb and Dumber, and Most Egregiously Stupid. It's rape. Child rape. Three little girls. Make it stop!

I have to remember that all I have to endure is the knowledge of what is happening. These little girls have the endure the actual pain. The fear. The sadness of being hurt by someone, for no reason. I feel like Shirley Maclaine in Terms of Endearment. She screams at the nurse "Someone help my daughter, she's in pain, give her the shot, she waited for four hours, someone help my daughter." I too want to scream "Someone help my granddaughters, its been going on long enough, they are hurt, they're in pain, someone help them." But no one helps. No one cares. No one listens. Everyone, and there have been multitudes of people I've contacted, tells me that its not their job, they don't do that, and I must contact someone else. No one is responsible for little girls being raped.

I have thought of killing Monster. But the police would surely rush to my home and arrest me. The police already told my son that they would arrest him if Monster was killed. Good to know. Protect him. But if I killed him, I would be in jail, fingerprinted, thrown in an orange jumpsuit, full throttle of the gendarmes against me, and locked up. But stopping a child rapist. That cannot be done. That they cannot and will not do.

Sadly, the girls have figured this out as well. They know that no one cares, and no one will make their pain stop.

I am horrified. Our country that claims to be the country of freedom. That children will grow up in safety. No one is allowed to terrorize a child. My granddaughters live in fear and pain.

Maybe instead of trucking around the world and fighting every known and unknown monster out there, we should first fight the real monsters right here at home. The monsters that rape little girls. Just a thought.

# Chapter 8 - Dr. Dr. Please

In 2009, my son went to court with his attorney's brother, who was also an attorney, to keep fighting for the girls. The mother was just determined she would have the children with the sex offender. She often petitioned the court that he was not a sex offender, and she wanted the children with him. Why didn't the judge see this? She's begging to have a sex offender, who rapes the kids, with the kids!

Keep in mind at this time, there is a court order that Monster Thomson, Monster, can have no contact with the children. No contact.

The regular attorney had told my son that he should have a court appointed psychologist to evaluate the families and the children. He said that when it is determined that the children are being violated, that a psychologist will always suggest that the children should not be with the person who is allowing it, and change custody. So my son felt that this was very important. The mother petitioned the court that my son should have no visitation, and not see the children.

So it was determined that day that the children and the families would be evaluated by a psychologist. My son did not know a psychologist, and the lawyer that came that day only wanted money. My son had paid and paid and paid the regular attorney, his brother, but all this attorney wanted on this day was money. "Have you got $100? Have you got anything?" My son said he wanted to empty his pockets and scream........

So my son went into the corridor of the court room and asked another attorney he knew if he knew of a psychologist who could interview everyone. That attorney gave my son a name of a psychologist, and my son presented that to the judge.

As I recall my son had to pay $12,000 for this consultation. Money is the key for everyone in the system. They can feel for you, and tell you they do, but show me the money is the name of the game. I know my son spent well in excess of $70,000 on lawyers, psychologists, and everything else for court.

My son, his girls, the mother, the grandparents and the sex offender were all to be evaluated for their safety to be around the children. Obviously the person that was most in need of evaluation was the sex offender. His lawyers regularly refused to have him evaluated. He in fact, hired the one lawyer who represented children in sex offender cases. How's that for disgusting? This big fat, ugly, disgusting little pig coming into court to see that nothing was said about him. Talk about insanity.

The sex offender was also offered up by Scary Mommy's lawyer, but the sex offender never presented himself to anyone. He ran. He hid. And all of Devil's family and friends came into court and lied and hid him. So he could rape and abuse the children. Yes I have died and gone to hell.

The sex offender refused to be evaluated. The psychologist notes in her report, that she was notified of his refusal. Let's remember that Devil is a very tactful liar, and pretty much everything she said to the psychologist and the courts, were lies.

Also in the psychologist's report, Devil said many interesting things. That Monster was not a sex offender, that she feels very strongly for Monster but would have no contact because she is not taking any chance of losing her kids, that she would play it on the safe side, and that she didn't want her children to be mentally abused by their father like she was. What? Wasn't the only person she respected enough and trusted enough to watch over the children in her absence, or with the Daddy, her father? So many lies, its hard to keep them all straight.

The psychologist determined it critical to evaluate Monster before having any more contact with the children.

With her father present, in another room, Layla told Dr. Judy that Monster was tall and fat having black hair. She said Monster hurt us, he put his penis in our chachi (private parts). Layla said their mommy was present at the time "outside" stating Monster did this only one time. The psychologist asked Layla if she told her mother and Layla stated, "Mommy doesn't listen." She doesn't want Monster in jail." Layla said Monster told her he was going to cut her hair if she told. Layla said Monster also, 'hit us with a bat on our bun. Layla said her mother told her, "Next time you tell you can get your hair all cut off." Layla said her mother and Monster, "They want to get married."

When Layla was with her mother.....Layla stated, "That stuff wasn't true, daddy made us tell you." Layla stated "Before we told him we loved Monster, he (daddy) slapped us." How do you slap a child before they tell you something. How do you know what they are going to say. Looks like Mommy told her to lie.

With her father present, in another room, Emily told Dr. Judy "Monster he sticked his finger in my chachi, and he had a friend "John" who watched. "Mom said not to tell anyone about Monster" She said "don't tell your dad, I don't want to go to jail." Emily also said Monster hit her with a paddle "after the shower." Emily said her dad,...."give me hugs, he plays with me." Emily said her mom lets Monster come around. Emily remarked "My mom really likes Monster. She wants to marry Clorey." Emily drew a series of pictures with various remarks including "I want to stop, Monster, he hurt my chachi." She also wrote, "No no no Monster. He hurt these people name Emily Layla Annie."

During the individual interview with the mother present in another room, Emily told this psychologist that when she was with dad, "he tell them to say Monster hurt them". Emily said that this was a lie. Emily did not elaborate, but said she likes visits with her dad stating they are good.

During Annie's interview, with the psychologist, and her father present in another room, Annie discussed Monster and described him as tall and fat having short black hair. Annie said she saw Monster "five days ago with my mommy." Annie stated "He put red stuff in his pee pee, put it in and touched it." Annie said this happened a long time ago. Annie said Monster spanked her with a bat on her butt and that "Papa John" (TJ) also spanked her. Annie said her mother, "She marries Monster. He's a bad guy. He has bad friends, They come over. They hurt our chachi (privates)." Annie said this happened "A long time ago. Mommy was at work." Annie said she told her mommy and stated "she said no." Annie said she saw Monster five days ago, with my mommy ' along with Layla and Emily.

During the interview with Annie with her mother in another room, Annie told this psychologist, "We told a lie about Monster and said her dad told them to lie. Annie stated "Daddy just told us so say that. Monster didn't do nothing." When asked about visits with their dad. Annie said "He always sings and talks to us."

The psychologist conducted an additional interview with the children escorted by their father. During individual interviews, Layla and Emily both denied anything happened with Monster and did not want to talk about him. Annie stated that she continues to see Monster stating, Annie talked about "Big Poppy" who she said dresses up like a woman because he doesn't want to be caught." The girls call Monster Big Poppy, which has always sickened me. It sounds like Sex Offender. Sorry. Big Poppy.

We had home interviews as well. In my home, in my son's home, and in Devil's mother Shorn's home. Layla said that grandma is "crabby" that she "hates you guys". Devil said that Layla was being mouthy and its not like her. She feels that the father "prepped" her. That has always just cracked me up. I know its sick for that to crack me up. But to blame Layla because your mother is a crab, and she hates you. I'd hate you too if you allowed your boyfriend, Big Poppy to molest me. Come on. Someone wake up. Anyone? I feel like this insanity has overtaken everyone.

The writing has been on the wall forever with this one. Sex offender. Girls making disclosures to everyone. Physical injuries at hospital. Monster is a sex offender. Monster Thomson is a sex offender. I mean come on.

Cloudy skies, thunder clouds, sirens going off....its going to rain.......logical thinking. No we'll have none of that.

At the time of these interviews, Monster Thomson, Monster, was to have no contact. No contact. It's all just unfathomable to me. But welcome to the court system.

I'm not sure that the advent of Dr. Judy was a good thing or a bad thing. Monster needed to be evaluated and that was a condition of the court. But he never came forward. He hid. In Oklahoma, in Florida, wherever. Then he'd come back and rape the girls. And no one cared. Devil's family always conspired to see that Monster had his victims. One Thanksgiving my son picked up the girls at Devil's mother's house. The girls were so upset because he was there, and he was being mean to them. Her family did not care what he did to them. And they had no desire to follow the court order "No Contact." Maybe they were too stupid to know what it meant.

The girls told us that their mother took them to talk to Dr. Judy, and cried all the way there. (It was about an hour trip for her.) The girls said she would say "If you tell Dr. Judy that Monster hurts you, then Mommy will go to jail, and I don't want to go to jail. You don't want your own Mommy in jail, do you? Who would take care of you." Is there anything more disgusting or revolting in this world for a Devil Mother to say than "let him rape you, or I'll be sad." What kind of a mother says this? Telling your children that they are being raped by your sex offender boyfriend, so that you can have this Monster in your life, and that is what makes her happy!

Just monstrous. Unbelievable. She knew. She knew everything. I have tried to wrap my brain around her thinking but it just won't happen. I'd kill someone who hurt my children. And she is grooming her children to be prostitutes for a sex offender! She told the girls if they lied, and nothing happened to Monster, she would take them to Toys R Us, and buy them new toys. They even told their dad about the toys they purchased. This is beyond any human decency. It sounds like a pimp, setting up a young girl.......buy her something nice, so she'll like it, and then pimp her out. And I imagine she got a Louis Vuitton bag, or a new Lexus, or a trip somewhere. Disgusting.

Dr. Judy initially seemed to really care about the girls, and they loved her. They loved anyone who showed them kind attention. They had a Devil mother who sold them out to a sex offender, and it showed on their little bodies. And their little minds. Their little minds were so damaged. And their little bodies hurt. They were so hurt and confused, and they didn't know where to turn or what to do. They were so smart and brave to tell us, but no one came to their rescue. No one. Which to me is pure insanity. And almost a more egregious fault than what the Devil and Monster were doing to them. They are three beautiful little girls, who deserve so much more. To be loved, to be protected, to not be harmed, to be treasured.........

The girls often told me that their mother slapped them, hit them, yelled at them, brushed their hair so hard they their heads hurt and they'd cry.....she was so mean to them. But put her in front of someone, and she'd lie and act her ass off. And Monster.....well everyone knows what a sex offender does. Except anyone in this case who should be helping little girls. No one came forward and fought for these little girls. We screamed, we yelled, we begged, we wrote letters, we called people......no one came forward.

My absolute favorite part of Dr. Judy's experience was Monster Thomson calling Dr. Judy and saying "I'm not a sex offender, that's not true. Where in the hell did that come from?" Uh, it came from the police department. Your conviction number is 96JD118. Don't you remember it? All of the police remembered it. Monster said he actually had no idea where that information came from. Well, Monster, you're as good of a liar as Devil. It happened to you when you were almost 18. I think most people have a cognitive memory at 18. Sex offender. You are a sex offender. Wear that badge proudly. It is who you are. I'm going to make t shirts that say "Monster Thomson is a sex offender." That's what he is. And for the courts not to use that knowledge to help little girls, and I'm talking little girls, is just so negligent and reprehensible. Who in

86

that courthouse, among the judges and lawyers would like their little girls to be with a sex offender? None of this would happen to them I'm sure. They'd be treated differently than we were.

Another time Monster Thomson sex offender Monster called Dr. Judy and threatened her. To the point that she was so fearful of him that she advised our attorney if she were to interview him, if he allowed that, that it would be at the courthouse with police presence. Yet this monster was with my granddaughters all the time. If this was her honest opinion, that she, a grown professional woman could not be safely with him, then why are my granddaughters with him? Raping them, hurting them, hitting them, terrifying them. What in this world is going on?

People in positions of power need to take a look at what is happening when little girls safety and lives are at stake. It's a horror movie everyday for these little ones. Everyday.

The children drew pictures for Dr. Judy to show what happens to them when they are with Monster. She sent us copies for our records, I guess in hopes they would help. Why didn't she present these to the courts? Unbelievable. They are drawings of little children being raped. One has a man's penis going into a little girl. The words say "No, no no Monster. He hurt these people names Emily, Layla, Annie". And "I want to stop Monster he hurt my chachi." Any questions? I believe its pretty clear. It's been pretty clear for a long time. Little girls drawing pictures, begging for help. No help ever came.

The most important thing I have learned. The courts will not help you. Devil was to produce Monster for evaluations with Dr. Judy. Never done. Monster was to come to court and get on the stand. Devil's attorney promised him in court. Never happened. Monster was to have no access to the children. Was with them all the time.

The truth had no place in the process. The truth didn't matter.

# Chapter 9 - Not the chosen one

During the three years we were in court fighting for the children's safety, I wrote to many people. I always felt that somehow, someway, someone would see what was happening and have a heart for three little girls.

I wish I had my old computer still. It died. Within that computer were all the letters I had written searching for help. And there were many. I wrote to Governor Quinn, asking for help. I still have a copy of that letter. I would also email him on his web site. I finally received a Doesn't care about the rape or trafficking of little girls. I contacted the President, Governors, Police agencies, the FBI, on and on and on. No one cared. No one.

My favorite was former President Bill Clinton. Someone I had sort of defended. I felt that as a President, you are basically a businessman. If you are intelligent, and you have the ability to manage and handle affairs (sorry) then you should be able to help someone in distress. I wrote to him several times. No reply. He had time for his side affairs, but not for me.

Then I saw in the news where he brought back Lisa Ling's sister from another country!! Went to another country to fight for her rights. But refused to even contact me or help me with three little girls being raped and molested and terrorized in the United States.

That is when I fully realized how little I mattered. I think I probably always knew, but never had to face it. I had no pull, no power. I could not call anyone to help me. There would be no big news for my little girls I guess.

If I were Lisa Ling, or someone famous, who could bring in headlines for someone, then maybe I'd matter.

But for now, no cigar.

I have no faith in anyone really.

I contacted President Barack Obama when he was still my senator asking for help. I received letters saying "Do you still need our help?" I'd resend the information, and nothing ever came. Everything regarding the girls was archived when he became President. Archived? These girls aren't dead. They're alive, and still being raped! Are you serious?

# Welcome to my nightmare.

It never ends.

Beautiful little girls
Playing, laughing,
always smiling and laughing,
vibrant, beautiful, adorable.
Lights of my life,
funny, adorable, sweet and dear.

To have your lives
Torn, ripped, destroyed
By your own mother.

Such a horrible destiny
Such a sad fate
We love you,
We pray that one day
you will be saved
From the hell that you
have been placed in

By your mother
By your grandmother Fern
By your very own family
Who loves a sex offender

We love you
We miss you
We pray that you are saved
And that you are
Safe

# Chapter 10 - Running with the Devil

One evening for no reason, my son Mick and I were on the computer. I had started looking at facebook, and reading different people's facebook entries. We were finding things out about people. To the point that we really wondered why the police or states attorney hadn't researched facebook. Most notably, because they didn't care.

We found Monster's facebook page. On this facebook were many very interesting posts. On January 14, 2009, Devil posted to Monster

"Open your eyes man!!! Let me guess, smoke in the eye??? Ha ha.....I love you baby and miss you very much!!! I don't want to escape, I like being in Hawaii with you." Where are the girls.......in Hawaii.......so again, trafficking the children.

On January 14, 2009, Eliza Chizer, aka Rocksy, states

"MT!!!!, so she's his friend as well. And she's not terribly prolific.

On January 15, 2009, Devil Devil states "hey baby....I love you!!! Miss you bunches and bunches."

During this time the court order says that Devil cannot live with Monster, and the children shall have no contact, all of these remarks are placed on their facebook. (I guess the police, the FBI, the states attorney's office didn't know how or didn't care to check into this. They haven't learned about computer's yet.) In January the posts regarding the "engagement" began showing up on Monster's facebook. Engaged to the Monster who rapes her kids.

Stephanie Soles Bead "I see you are engaged! Congrats!" January 16, 2009

Melody Wene Koles "Congrats on the engagement tell Devil I said hello, haven't seen her in like 10 years! January 16,2009

Karen Coop Wheels "Congrats on the engagement! That's great!"

January 17, 2009

Devil Mazur "Can I just tell you how lucky I feel to be your girl!! I love it and love you so much. The most amazing man I have ever met!! January 18 2009

The most amazing man she's ever met is a sex offender who is court ordered to have no contact with her children, and she has trafficked her children to him, let me repeat that again, she has trafficked her children to him in Texas, against court order!!!!!!!

Devil Fender "Congratulation on your engagement!" January 22, 2009

Devil Mazur "I love you baby!!! It is almost done!" April 25, 2009

Such a celebratory mood. "It" is lying to the courts in Illinois and trafficking her children to Monster in Texas. The final court date for disposition of the case was April 29, 2009.

And the weeks before she and the Monster had gone to Texas to rent an apartment so they could traffick the children to Texas. How did they know what the outcome of the case was to be?

Devil Mazur to Monster Thomson "You are so handsome, I just want to eat you up!!" July 18, 2009 She wants to eat up the sex offender!

Mary Ann Belch "Wat r u doin to Devil she looks happy and healthy? Soo happy for u all. August 9, 2009

Mary Ann Belch "Wats up Monster? Hows Devil and the girls?"

September 15, 2009 Maria apparently can't spell.

Devil Mazur to Monster "I love you so much! You make me a better person and I love you for that! How did I become so lucky to get a man like you!!??!!" January 20, 2010

(Just a guess, but I think the answer is that he's a pedophile and you have three little girls. I don't think its love.)

And my personal favorites:

"Monster, any time you want to chat with me you know I am here!!!" January 29, 2010 by Fern, maternal grandmother of the children!!!!

Do you need to discuss why your grandchildren are across several state lines against court order with the sex offender?

Fern "Thank you for taking such good care of my girls.....Love Fern" February 14, 2010

Why is the sex offender taking care of the girls against a court order? Why is this alright with the maternal grandmother?

My granddaughters don't have a chance in hell. Their mother, their mother's friends, their maternal grandmother, their families are all willing to say to hell with the court order, and expose these children to the sex offender no matter what! No matter what the costs to the children. To the point that the mother trafficks them from Illinois to Texas, and the entire group lies in court against the little girls!!! I just don't get it. I really don't get it.

The following all posted on February 18, 2010. And this post is by Monster Thomson sex offender, Monster:

"Kudos to you, Illinois and all of your law enforcement agencies, for allowing psychotic criminals to live in your state and not pay child support, threaten law abiding citizens and accuse people of unthinkable thing. What a joke he makes out of all of you! Grow a sac!"

The above paragraph has always just crippled me, and made me wonder where I am living. Certainly not in America. This is a sex offender who has trafficked three little girls, against court orders, from Illinois to Texas, (and Brazil, Hawaii, Oklahoma) with the complete simpatico of the mother, Devil, her family, her friends, and lying repetitively to the courts, and they are getting away with it. No one cares. No one reads it. No one goes after him. He is trafficking children across state lines for the purpose of having sex with them, and making it known to everyone, and no one cares............beyond anything I can even imagine.......and its working for them!!!!!!

Please know that the words and spelling are not mine, but the person who posted this vile. In response to Monster's post:

Responses:

**Emmy Shires "Gee Monster, anybody specific in mind. Lol" 2/18/2010**

**Teresa Ryan "I hope everything is okay." February 18, 2010**

**Jon Tough "That's the system for ya. Fucking bullshit!!!!"**

**Loren Queen "Must be a fuckin loser"**

**Crys Lyman "I have to agree this state is definatley screwed up"**

**Devil Mazur Couldn't have said it better myself. Love you honey!!!**

**Kimmy Curse "Its just sad that someone has to be forced to take care of their kids. He should want to make sure his children have what they need instead of another man doing it for him."**

**Lori G. "Tell them like it is Monster its sad."**

**Jennifer M. " He is gross!!"**

No actually all of you are idiots. Everything that is said in this despicable language, and clear class of ignorance is almost embarrassing. These are misinformed, ignorant, people in their early thirties carrying on against a man who is trying to protect his little girls. And Monster is all the while, proud to show that he is disobeying the courts orders that he have no contact with these children. He is declaring a father fighting for his girls as a piece of trash. The mother trafficked them to him illegally, and all of their ignorant friends are carrying on like freaking morons. And I'd like to add that the ignorance and misspelling is exactly as it shows on the facebook page. Just beyond disgusting. And all of these friends are aware that Monster is to have no contact with the children. What kind of people are these monsters?

I know my granddaughters are surrounded by morons, with no concern for what is right and wrong. They are listening to a sex offender and an apologist for a sex offender, and are showing how very ignorant they are. I know my granddaughters really don't have a chance. They cannot buy a chance. And the ignorance as well goes to Fern the maternal grandmother who was in court when the court order was handed down regarding the danger of the pedophile. No contact. No contact. No contact. And she and her family allowed him contact whenever he wanted it, to the point of trafficking them to Texas!!!

Also on Monster's face book we also found these postings. Someone in the Monster, Devil camp had found a newspaper article, very small, one paragraph, regarding my son Mick, the girls' father. It said that my son had been pulled over because his truck had out of state plates, and wasn't properly registered to him.

It was about three in the morning and he was really tired. The local police feared he may have stolen the vehicle as it was registered to a name in another state. The problem was that my son hadn't switched over the registration yet. It was all ended with no problems.

One of the "friends" of Monster and Devil posted it to Monster's facebook. Among the responses were the following: again not my words,

Monster Thomson, Monster "FATHER OF THE YEAR CANDIDATE! "

Jason Reid "I have seen you talk about this guy a few times. Who the fuck is he?" (This one is beyond disgusting. He is their father.)

Monster Thomson "My fiances' ex. A punk-ass bitch who I hope got raped in jail. He went to Mac because they kicked him and his hillbilly family out of Hercher". (Am I crazy, isn't hoping rape upon little girls' father, that you have taken illegally across state lines, a really odd hope?)

Jason Reid "Sounds like a douche, Anyone with children who does the stiff you listed needs to get sawed in half." (The person who is illegally with the children is Monster, your friend.)

Monster Thomson "That's why we always got alone so well Jason, we are so much alike and have the same opinion on people who deserve to die. Ask anyone who has ever know the scumbag and they will say the same thing. In the end we all get what's coming to us, right?!?" (Monster Thomson, Monster was to be evaluated by a psychiatrist before having any contact with the three minor children, for good reason. He's a pedophile. His words give him away.)

Monster Thomson "LOVE THIS POST! MY FAVORITE OF ALL TIME I COULD READ IT OVER AND OVER." (Loves knowing that pain is being caused to the children's father.)

96

Jason Reid "Yeah we always got along great. I am a person of love but also person that believes in bashing in skulls if one is deemed worthy, At least you don't live in the same state as him and have to deal with him on a daily basis." (No, Monster ran to Texas, and Devil brought the children to him, against court order.)

Devil Mazur "I have to say it makes me smile a little too!!!"

Eliza Chizer "Karma's a bitch MT!!! This is what he gets....he fucks himself every time. J I understand he makes you madder than mad, but everyone knows you're a good man, I love ya~~~"(no he's not a good man, he's a sex offender)

And most oddly this one that really creeped me out.

Monster Thomson, "Hey Matt, When he back off the pink just because of the stink,....Summers Eve.....Douche! If he holds his nose when you take of your pantyhose....Summers Eve......Douche~"

Am I crazy? Aren't these really odd words for a sex offender? Aren't his responses to the father of the children he's raping really out there? Aren't their friends just nuts? I can't imagine any friend I ever had, dragging her children across the country to place children with a sex offender. Against court orders!!! And all their friends chiming in with the sex offender!!!!It's more despicable than anything I've ever heard.

And then Eliza Chizer and Chrissy Cheese follow up this disgusting tirade with:

"I hope he doesn't karate chop me in the neck.

I'm karate CHOPPING ALL OF YOU!!!!"

My granddaughters being sexually trafficked around the country to a sex offender is a form of entertainment for these creeps. And they have the nerve to say anything negative towards my son, the father of three little girls who are being raped!!! I just bleed for my granddaughters. I know that their pain is so horrific. No one will listen, and no one will care.

Oddly I had decided to do a search for Monster Thomson, Monster on the internet. I knew in my gut I would find him with the children. I honestly can't remember which came first. The website search, or happening onto facebook. However, I paid for a search and found that Monster Thomson was living in Conroe, Texas. I then called the police in Conroe Texas to see if they could help me. I wanted to let them know that a sex offender, and his Devil, had taken my granddaughters to Texas against an Illinois court order. I did not know the proper etiquette for someone defying a court order. I felt that just bringing it to the attention of the authorities would bring it all out in the open, and the girls hell would stop.. We in fact had a letter from Lisa D. State Representative, that stated when and if we found out the court order was not being followed, we should bring that to the attention of the authorities. So I did.

Mr. Glissen, the policeman, went to the address we had found. We wanted to know if the children were on a lease with him. Oddly enough it wasn't until a few days later that I realized that Devil was on the lease with him. So Deputy Glissen would go to that address and see if the children were on the lease with Monster.

And indeed, he found that the girls were on the lease. All five of them were on a lease together. I found this lease by searching a website. When the Devil mother had gone to court for permission to move the children out of state, we knew she would traffick them to Monster Thomson Monster. She had no money to live on. She never worked, except sparingly and would usually get fired. So we knew when she asked the courts permission to move away from Illinois, and that the father should not see the children for two years, that she was lying to everyone. Our worst fears had been confirmed. We had not known from April 2009, until January 2010 where the girls even were.

They were in Conroe, Texas with the sex offender, that the court order stated they could have no contact with. And the mother was not to live with him, nor were the children. Crossing state lines with children for the purpose of having illegal sex. And no one will do a thing.

Deputy Glissen contacted the judge to give her his information.

The judge left the case. In her departure she stated on the paperwork "the court received ex parte communications which directly impact the credibility of the witnesses at the hearing on the petition to remove." Devil and her witnesses lied to have the children taken out of state to live with the sex offender, and after three years in court trying to save his daughters, they were now with the sex offender, against court orders. So much for the truth, the whole truth, and nothing but the truth. In this case it has been lies, total lies, and nothing but lies. And it has served the sex offender and the lying mother well.

And no one cared. And no one was willing to do a thing.

Monster and Devil should have been brought back to Illinois and arrested.

No, nothing. Little girls do not matter.

My blood boils when I think of this.

The courts. The truth, nothing but the truth, so help you God......no. It was lies, nothing but lies......and no one did a thing about all the lies that were told to place little girls with a sex offender.

Am I in America? It doesn't seem at all right to me. It seems totally un American.

We had to start completely over with a new lawyer, a new judge, all new. And there was nothing that would be done to the Devil or the Monster for trafficking these little girls.

My son had to begin all over again, and know that basically his children were out of the state, with the sex offender, and our time was over. The worst that could have happen indeed did happen.

# Chapter 11 - Welcome to my nightmare

A date with destiny, April 29.

The girls initially told us their horror story of sexual abuse by Monster on April 29, 2007. The final court date, regarding their custody, happened to fall on April 29, 2009. This date is my youngest son Teddy's birthday.

The girls knew they were going away. They kept telling us that Monster and Devil were going to find a place to live, and when they came back they would move. And they said they'd never see us again. It upset them, and obviously upset us.

Devil left the girls with Mick for about ten days before the final court date regarding custody, April 29, 2009. I guess when you're fearful of the father hurting the children, or running off with the children, you leave them with him while you look for a place to live with a sex offender. Against court orders. Across state lines. Then you go into court and get yet another order of protection. Lying is all Devil has ever known how to do. She's a pro.

The girls kept telling us that they would be leaving and they would miss us. They started leaving little notes all over the house that said "I love you Mim, I love you Papa," or "I'll miss you Daddy." "Good bye. Don't forget me." They had been telling us for months that they'd be leaving, but we didn't know where or when.

My son finally decided with a tad of coaxing by me, that we should make a DVD of the girls for the courts. The girls had regularly begged their dad to talk to the judge. Mick had told them that a judge was hearing everything regarding Mommy, Daddy and Monster, and would make a decision for the girls so they would be safe. We thought this was the right thing to do. The girls often begged their father to talk to the judge. They wanted to tell her what Monster did to them, how scared they were of him, how Mommy made them be with him, how no one would help them. The judge refused this. So my son put each one of them in front of his camera and filmed them asking for help. Saying what Monster does to them, and that they don't like it. He felt if the girls disappeared he would have this to show to someone, and possibly get help for the girls. The girls would ask their daddy and me if we could kill Monster, or get someone to kill him to make it stop. It was all very terrifying to us. These little girls left us and went back to a hell, where they were raped, not only by a sex offender, but by his friends. His disgusting friends. And beaten. Ruthlessly beaten and hit and hurt, and carved on. It was horrific. And they left in fear. Unhappy and scared.

The girls each made their own section of the DVD with their dad in the room. No one else. He wanted to be sure they each spoke their own truth, and didn't act off what the others said. After it was all done, the twins asked me if I'd watch it with them. I thought that was odd. I said "I'm not sure I want to watch it." They both looked at me and said "Please watch it Mim, we'll watch it with you." I don't know if they had a strange fascination with what they'd said, or why they wanted to see it, but we put the DVD in and turned it on. The girls said things so horrific, that I'd never heard before. I would turn to look at them with my eyes bulging out, in complete shock, and they would turn to me and shake their heads yes, as if to say "Yes, Yes this is happening to us." These little girls were desperate for someone, anyone to know what was happening to them. And for someone to intercede. It was all very sad. I now believe they wanted me to see it, and hear it, and know how horrific their lives had become. They told many things, that I'd never heard before. My heart and my mind ached. My heart was literally broken. I could feel just horrific pains in my chest.

At the next to last court date, when the girls fate would be determined, Mick had brought the DVD to give to his lawyer. The opposing counsel, Grodey, had his eye on the DVD that sat atop Mick's lawyers books. Mick's lawyer felt he should see it first before disclosing it to anyone. And Mick made is as a sort of safeguard in case the girls did disappear. Grodey starting asking what the DVD was, and what it was about, and why doesn't Mick give it to your honor to see. So after much deliberation, between Mick and his lawyer, they decided to give it to the judge.

They just went on to say that there was no proof that Monster was with the children. And after that I couldn't tell you one thing she said because my mind exploded. I believe 96JD118 says it all.

The court dates were hell. The judge never cared or listened.

Sadly, I read in the paper this very day, about a local attorney who told of his court experience with a local judge, and I quote "We lawyers often complain that when we go to different counties, local lawyers get preferences in decision, rulings, schedule dates and overall convenience. This is called getting "homered".

We were indeed homered. After my son's first lawyer Kim left the case,( because she gave information to a police officer,) he had hired a Chicago lawyer that I had found. (Oddly, we later learned that this lawyer had written a grandparents law for the state of Illinois. Our judge had also written one, but hers wasn't chosen. So game on. Sadly, he was not happy with him.) I do feel he was "homered"........which to me a lawyer admitting is the case, is just profoundly disgusting. I thought being a lawyer was all about truth, and dignity, and fairness. What a crock. It's about being on the home team.

We knew this. Devil's lawyer Grodey, was a pig. He had to weigh 400 pounds. He lumbered about. He was disgusting. Not because he was fat, because he was disgusting. I've known overweight people who are not disgusting. Just giving a visual. The things he said were disgusting. My son always remembers one day when the judge couldn't find her pen, and Grodey went up on the dais, and got on all fours and crawled under her desk to retrieve her pen. They giggled and laughed. My son could not believe what he was seeing. I believe he made a remark to the judge. I'm overweight. You won't find me crawling under anyone's desk.

The first date the girls told of us the sexual abuse was April 29, 2007. Although there had been hints of it before, this was the first time they discussed it with us. Our final court date for the disposition regarding the custody of the girls was April 29, 2009.

We were really nervous. The day started very oddly. This day is easy to remember as it is my youngest son Teddy's birthday.

A letter written April 28, 2009 from the Illinois Department of Children and Family Services, was special delivered to our home, early in the morning of April 29, 2009, when we were preparing to leave for court. The letter read as follows:

**Michael Thomas**

**Re: NOTICE OF FORBIDDEN ACCESS TO STATE PROPERTY**

**Mr. Thomas,**

**You are hereby notified that you are forbidden from entering the State of Illinois Department of Children and Family Services field office located at 505 S. Schuyler, Kankakee, Illinois 60901, effective IMMEDIATELY, and continuing until further notice.**

**Please be advised that any violation of this Notice will result in law enforcement being notified and possible charges for Criminal Trespass to State Supported Land pursuant to 710 ILCS 5/21.5**

**Sincerely,**

**Claire Tiffany**

**DCP Supervisor**

To receive this letter as we were readying ourselves to go to the courthouse, was daunting. It told a story, indeed. DCFS, Claire Tiffany, who had never met the children, and Bob Leonard, were firmly in Devil's pocket, regardless of what information they received or what happened to the children. Claire Tiffany actually got on the stand early on and said "I've never met the children." It was insidious. They never looked at what was happening to the children. They didn't care.

We tried to gather ourselves and head to the courthouse. My son had repeatedly begged the people at DCFS for help, and no help ever came. Many people had told us that DCFS doesn't care about children. As long as they have a roof over their head, a meal to eat, and a bed to sleep in, they do not intervene. Too much work. And I believe it. Look up DCFS on the internet and see the horror stories. It's disgusting.

But we went on to court.

When we went for the final court date, it was like a dark cloud had descended upon us. I cannot begin to describe what it felt like. Death. The foyer of the very old, very distinct, really beautiful, strikingly against the reality of what we were facing. The foyer was also oddly empty. On one side of this huge space was Devil and her family, laughing, almost jovial. A stark contrast to our fears and worries. Again, no Monster. He was safely hidden away thanks to the efforts of Devil and her family and friends. They did his dirty work for him. On the other side was me, my husband, my son and his then girlfriend, Jess. We still had some silly hope that some way, somehow, something would go right for the girls.

The waiting in the foyer went on and on and on. Seemed like forever. It was at this time that a new man was working the foyer, was in the foyer glad handing and speaking to everyone. Not to us of course, but to everyone else. Devil, Shorn, Floyd, Sorry, Rocksy, Sorry's sorry husband, TJ, Devil's family, the police personnel that were there......happy......no worries. They were all laughing and trading quips and smiling. While we were quiet and scared. When we got to the courthouse I saw a man that really grabbed my curiosity. I kept looking at him. Wondering. The waiting in the foyer seemed like forever. Finally it hit me. I realized the man in the suit and the moustache, that we'd never seen before was indeed Uncle Ernie. The Uncle Ernie that the girls say molests them, puts his bat in them, parks his police car in the garage, has radios on so he can know where the police are, kisses them, dropped Emily on her head. Emily showed me the bruise on her head she had a few weeks earlier. She said Uncle Ernie was messing with her. She said Uncle Ernie comes over all the time and hurts her. She lifted her newly cut bangs and showed us the bruise on her forehead. A large sizable bruise. Emily had never had bangs before. Much like Annie's haircut we saw on Monster's website. All the threats "do you want me to cut your hair?" came true for Annie. Her hair was barely an inch all over her head. It previously, when she was around us, was very long. It kept getting shorter, and shorter, and shorter.

For Mick and I this came down on us like a lead balloon. I told Mick, "that's Uncle Ernie." He said "Are you sure? I said "I'm sure." I can't begin to tell you how hard of a reality this was for Mick and myself. The girls had told us this name over and over and over again. We had not connected the Ernie Thomson, to the chief of police of Manteno, ever. It sort of landed again, like a lead balloon. I knew Mick was dying inside. I know I was. To learn this as we stood on the precipice of entering the courtroom doors, with all the gendarmes ready to pounce, was a really tough foreboding. It took our breath away. This is the man that rapes our granddaughters, while wearing a badge. With his police car in the garage. With radios on so he can answer any calls in case something should go wrong. It's really more than our minds could take in. This man was on task forces for the entire county.

This descended on Mick like a death knoll. He asked me several times "Are you sure?" How do you know?"

I said "The girls told me that Uncle Ernie hurts them. When I knew there was indeed an Uncle Ernie, I looked up Ernie on the internet, and found a picture. That is the man in the picture. That's the man. Remember Layla's description. " Kind of fat, kind of shorter than Monster, a little mustache, he wears a badge, and he drives a cop car." Layla even described the cop car for us. I honestly was afraid for Mick's mind at this time. It was such a huge blow to take before having to walk in and face the gendarmes that were running the show.

Mick fell apart inside himself. He was so hurt. Here is the man that girls have spoken of. The man that they say hurts them. The man named Ernie that threatens to kill their Daddy. And here he was glad handing everyone in the court house foyer. Here he was chatting with Devil's lawyer. Here he was shaking hands with and practically dancing with the Judge. He actually gave the judge a sort of low five as they passed in the corridor and chuckled. He did this about five feet from us, and it was obviously for show. He smiled right at us. He was reveling in his role, whatever it was that day, and revealing to us his mite.

We all had a horrible sinking sick feeling. We felt things would not go well at all. We were sunk even further when Mick's lawyer was called into a private meting with Grodey and the judge.

He was Ernie Thomson. The girls had told us that "Uncle Ernie" hurt them. So we had wondered if that Ernie was Ernie Thomson.....as Monster's last name was Thomson. Ernie Thomson was the chief of police of Manteno, Illinois, where the police earlier had threatened and terrified a private detective. So all of my antenna were up. Our antenna were up whenever we were in this courthouse. The mother, who sexually trafficked the children to the sex offender, always had police protection. This day was no different. Ernie Thomson was glad handing everyone including the judge. Devil's family was all grouped together with Grodie and Ernie gathered with them sporadically and they'd laugh and point things out to each other. They were jovial. We were fearful. It felt as though we were being led into a death chamber. To the slaughter. I know my son and I felt like we were in a death grip. He was falling apart inside. The man who rapes your kids, is in court to claim them. To claim them for Monster. We heard different things through our attorney. Ernie had been to DCFS to watch the DVD that my son made. Why? If Ernie had been named as a suspect, why wasn't he investigated? Why was he here? What in the hell was going on? I had never in my life gone to the police to ask for help with anything. Why didn't someone, do something, to help innocent little girls.

At some point Grodey, our attorney and the judge went into chambers, for what we did not know. After awhile, Grodey came out practically dancing with papers in his hand. Our attorney looked like he had been smacked in the face. Mick's lawyer actually told him and us that we didn't have to come into the courtroom to hear the decision. We could wait outside. My son had waited over three years for this decision. He would be in the court room.

It took about an hour after the meeting before we all went in to the courtroom. When we did, there were probably three or four very large police officers standing around my son. They had their fists on their hips. Like they were ready. They always stood around him as a form of intimidation. I did not know where Ernie Thomson was until later. We sat for a short while before the judge began. She started with the DVD that my son had made with the girls. He made this as the girls wanted to tell the judge that they were scared, and that Mommy was going to take them away to live with Monster. They did not want to go. The judge had taken that DVD in a previous court date, after Grodey made demands that it be turned over to the court. The judge claimed she watched it and that the girls had been coached to say what they said, and that she did not believe it. Never mind that the girls had physical injuries to concur with their words, and that Dr. Kruzak's testimony matched their words. The judge did not care.

Devil had regularly put in court papers that she wanted the children to live with Monster. She repeatedly requested this. So of course, everyone knew, given any chance to take the children out of state, that she would take them to Monster. Except the Judge. The judge wrote that the mother could take the children to live out of state, and keep the location secret from the father. So, the judge helped Devil traffick the children to Monster. She took three beautiful little girls who had told two DCFS officers, an emergency room physician, two nurses, a grandmother, a father, a friend, that they were being raped by Monster, a sex offender, and by others; and handed them over to him on a silver platter. Why did we ever go to court and believe they would help? We were stupid. We were really stupid. Courts screw little kids. They don't help them.

108

She went on to say that my son made it all up, and made the girls say it. Excuse me, At one point Layla says "Daddy what's that guys name?" Mick, cautiously says "You mean Ernie", and she goes "No Monster." So if he was coaching, they weren't listening. I will never forget Emily saying in a very sad soft voice....when asked by her father, "what is it you want to say to the judge?" Emily says "Help.....I'd say we need help." And the girls went on and on and on about everything Monster does to them. What he allows others to do to them. That these men ask Monster "how much will this cost?" They were just amazing in their strength telling what happened to them. They wanted to talk to the judge. They begged their daddy to let them talk to her. My son made this as his final statement, because in our hearts I believe we all knew that the judge was not going to rule for my son. But against us. And for the sex offender and scary Mommy.

Also I must add, as far as making it up, and coaching the girls.....these girls would do little shows for us for entertainment. They'd go in the kitchen and walk into the front room and tell a little story, or sing a little song, and then run from the room giggling from being nervous and embarrassed. In the DVD, they sat quietly, no giggling, no laughing and no nerves. Pleading for help.

These poor little girls had been asking for months to speak to the judge. They wanted to tell her that Monster never went away. That Mommy left them alone with Monster. That he let others hurt them. That they were scared and wanted it to stop. This was never allowed. We had been told repeatedly by so called "experts" that a judge will talk to the children, alone in cases such as this. She refused.

And that the children could go with the Devil, away for two years, and we would not know where they were. My son had not been arrested, nor had there been any police involvement in the past two years. How she came up with that one, I have no idea. Men in prison get to see their children. My son would not see his children for two years. Devil could get protective orders like buying gum. Remember that when the first investigation was going on she got an order of protection against my son, for the sex offender to be with the children. Amazing......just amazing. I don't think this judge had one clue what was going on. Not one. Or she was terribly corrupt. Whatever the situation was, she just enabled a very sick mother to traffick her children to a sex offender. And we knew it. And the children knew it. We later learned that a mother can practically kill her children, and the courts will still leave the children with the mother.

(Every lawyer my son has spoken with post trial cannot believe what they are told. When a doctor comes onto the stand and verifies rape by a sex offender, and that the mother willingly allowed it, the children are removed from her custody. Or so we were told.)

With that, in some sort of cerebral unison, Jess, my son's girlfriend, Mick and I stood, and walked out of the courtroom, with the thugs (armed huge police officers) on our tail. I remember just as she said these things, happiness and glee erupting from Devil's family, particularly her father TJ, who looked like he'd won the lottery. We just got up and starting booking it out of there. I felt the police on my heels. I felt them very strongly, to the point I could feel their breath on my back, and very profoundly heard the click of their shoes.......one of their hands went very securely into my back as I walked and they stated "get out of here before we cuff you and take you to jail." We were walking as fast as we could. It was obvious we were leaving the courthouse. As we left the courtroom, I remember Ernie Thomson, immediately outside the door of the courtroom, sitting in a chair at the very door, we practically had to step over him, smiling up at us, with a look of "f you"...and grinning like a Cheshire cat. Such a proud little creepy guy. "Lost your kids, eh sucker? You know what I do to them!"

I believe they wanted my son, or myself to become angry and say something so they could arrest one of us, and build a case against us. As if they hadn't already. They had built a case of b.s. that secured three little girls to a sex offender. It's just so frightening to remember all of this. Its abysmal. And the victims are little girls. The furor that was directed at us, was merely to keep the little ones in harms' way. I often wonder how they have survived.

The police officers were so close I could feel their breath on my neck. I could smell their aftershave. My husband was on the opposite side of the rotunda, and said it looked crazy. They were on our heels. We were walking as fast as we could. I wanted my son out of harms' way. The police had stood around him, muscled him pushed him around for three years. All in the name of the Devil and her sex offender. My personal favorite, is when Devil would come to court, and be in the basement, Then just before court, they'd bring her up in the elevator, with a police escort. She was fearful of my son. Sure? And I've got a bridge in New York I'd like to sell. My granddaughters are fearful of the men who rape them. Maybe one day someone will show some concern for three little girls. Three little girls.!!! We reached the exit, which was a revolving door. The large gloved hand on my back with the shove, was a very clear sign of intimidation. The three officers breathing down our neck was a very clear sign. Why was it necessary to chase us out of the courtroom? Why was this allowed? Why was Ernie right there watching? Smiling? Don't we have a right to leave the courtroom as we choose? Welcome to my nightmare.

Ernie and his thugs were here to protect Devil and serve the kids up to Monster. We have known this for some time. Having it shoved down our throats was another thing entirely. I felt like those movies you see when someone is in a third world country, accused of something ridiculous, and they are being hounded and treated like dirt by the courts. It was a feeling I could never fully impart to anyone. Scary. Terrifying. Horrifying. Out of body. I would feel this, and then realize that the real pain, the real horror, the real hell was actually upon three little girls. All this hell, all this interference, all the police doing their dirty work, for a sex offender to be able to terrorize, traffick and terrify three little girls. They just happened to be my granddaughters. That I loved more than anything in this world. And indeed the Devil immediately trafficked the children to Texas to the sex offender Monster.

Ernie Thomson came into court to vouch for these monsters who immediately trafficked the children to Texas. Does he have any liability?

We got out of the courthouse. My husband had remained in the courthouse rotunda while we went into the courtroom. The officers laughed and joked about us, and hoped that they had scared us sufficiently. I have never heard of people being chased out of a courtroom, and courthouse, by police officers and terrorized. Welcome to Kankakee. As I said before, immediately outside in the circle drive was a big security van to take people to jail. We were the only people in the courthouse at this time. I think the messages were very clear. Get out of Dodge. Don't pass go. Don't collect $200. Just get the hell out. And we did.

We left and went to my son's house. A police car followed us. We stopped at a Casey's store, and a police car was following us. Unbelievable. The gendarmes were on patrol. When we got to my son's we tried to talk and relive what had happened. We were all in shock as we remain today. Little girls being sexually trafficked by a woman and a man who are forbidden to be together. And the judge also allowed the mother Dirt, I mean Devil, to take the children out of state to an "undisclosed location" because she was so fearful of my son. Excuse me. She had left the children for ten days with my son before the court date. She had gone with the sex offender to find a place to live in another state, as we later learned. Fear? No fear. Just a good offense I guess.

I have a copy of her court order. I have a copy of everything as far as that goes. Devil lies, courts go with her. Devil lies, courts go with her. The following is the request for an order of protection against my son that she received for two years, and trafficked the girls out of state, with the father knowing nothing.

"He is constantly stalking me at my home. Following me when I drive & when I go places with my children & family. I am in fear for my children's my own safety. I fear he will kidnap my children. He has threatened to take them out of state w/me not getting a chance to even talk to the girls. After hearing him during these

112

court proceedings I feel he is delusional. I fear that he will snap at any moment & take the children or even kill them. & myself. He has no concept of realty. He has continually put my children through many unnecessary physical exams & continually talking to them about our "Adult" situations with court." (There is actually a period after kill them, which she thought better of and added a period & myself.) Have to make it look as threatening as possible.

The words and spelling above are Devil's, not mine. She is not terribly literate. Where is Devil's police reports to verify all of this. There are none. Following you where and when. If you are in fear of your children's safety, why did you leave the children with him for ten days while you and Monster went on a vacation together, just before the hearing. You kidnapped the children. You took them out of state, with the sex offender, against court orders, with the assistance of Ernie Thomson. My son having no chance to even talk to the girls. As far as being delusional, he is not, and you do not have the education to evaluate that for someone. I believe Devil barely graduated high school. She is certainly not capable of determining someone's mental capacities. As Dr. Judy states very clearly in her report, "Due to the unresolved issues and apparent risk factors presented with Devil's relationship with Monster Thomson, this psychologist recommends that Michael Thomas has legal rights to his children through Joint Custody. This psychologist believes Michael Thomas has legitimate concerns that if Devil was awarded primary physical and legal custody of their daughters, Devil would get married to Monster Thomson and possibly leave the state with no recourse on Mr. Thomas' part."Consistent with Partner Relational Problem, Michael presents with significant stress with his ex-wife including concerns regarding her boyfriend, Monster Thomson, an adjucated sex offender, who he fears may have continued access to his children through his ex wife. It is this psychologist's opinion that Michael's paranoia and fear in regards to Monster Thomson is based upon reality (and not a delusion) as Monster Thomson is reported to be an adjudicated sex offender and Devil admits she would like to continue her relationship with Monster and possibly get married to him in the future. " And indeed this is what happened.

Maybe Dr. Judy should've thought this through further. The custody went to the mother, who immediately trafficked them to the sex offender. I don't believe either judge ever read the psychologist's report which cost I believe in excess of $12,000. The courts. You came here looking for Justice? It's just us.

If you Devil fear that he will take them out of the state, why did you leave them alone with him for ten days while you went off with sex offender for ten days? As for the many unnecessary physical exams. There was one physical exam after the order was written that the children could not go to the doctor. My response to this directive is, where am I living? In Sudan? In a poor developing country? No I live in America. When children are sick, or have rape injuries, you take them to the doctor. This judge just gave Devil a home run with that b.s. When did doctor visits become something that is a dangerous thing for a little girl living with a sex offender? Am I nuts?

Devil had gone out of town with Monster over the New Years holiday. My son had the girls. Emily had suffered horribly with vaginal pain. She was seeping horribly. She could barely walk. Her dad carried her around, and she cried. She was miserable. They also kept telling their daddy that they were afraid, that Mommy and Monster were getting a place to live, and they were leaving soon. They didn't want to go.

My son, after much consternation, and agony, and trying to reach Devil, finally decided to take Emily to the hospital. All the same ingredients were present. Child in pain, vagina swollen and sore, terribly oozing, and in horrific pain. My son did not take the children to "numerous" hospital visits, although they surely needed a physician many times. We were unable to take them, as it was court ordered we could not. Their vaginas always looked horrific. I'm a woman, so I know that a vagina does not become irritated, turn inside out, turn beat red, and ooze unless something is terribly wrong. And if it hurts, you go to the doctor. Other than giving birth, and a few infections, I have never experienced this pain in my life. These little girls experienced it all the time! All the time. My son had to go to the store and buy Emily a new package of

114

underwear as all of her underwear was soaked with her oozing, sore, swollen private parts. So he took her to the hospital. Again, she told of being hurt. Again, nothing was done. The mother went to court and suspended my son's visitation because he took the child to the hospital. What's a father to do? Nothing. We virtually had our hands and our tongues tied. Let Monster rape them. She had very firmly accomplished her goals. Made way for the Monster. The Monster who was to be evaluated by the psychologist, the Monster who was to present himself to the court for his safety to be with the children evaluated, the Monster that hid and ran behind her skirt. The Monster that Devil, TJ, Shorn, Floyd, Rocksie, her dumb sister who's name I can't remember, as she is not at all memorable, and every other vegetable they were friends with, made way for Monster to have his meat. Disgusting is all I can say. He can't make it to court, but we'll get there for him and deliver his victims! Where's Tony Soprano?

So, after court, and being splayed open like a dead fish, we went to my son's house, on the edge of Kankakee. The girls had actually told us once, that the house they went to where men hurt them, was in an area where they could see Daddy's house out the back window. Amazing. So we tried to gather ourselves, and make sense out of what had all just conspired. We couldn't. We headed back home, to Watseka. Mick and Jess both came too. We felt we had escaped a shark that day, but knew the girls hadn't been so lucky. They were in the depths of hell. When we got home, Mick's lawyer from Chicago called me. He couldn't believe what had happened. He was basically shell shocked. He asked me lots of question, and I filled him in. He was stunned. He seemed as though he hadn't really listened or heard everything before. He couldn't believe everything I was telling him. We must have talked for over an hour. After I hung up with him, I got a call from the FBI. The FBI in Champaign, Illinois. They wanted to meet with us and talk to us, that night. I wasn't sure I could do it. We were shot. Shot and left for dead. Couldn't really believe that all of our work and concerns had ended in such a hell for the girls. We knew that Devil was going to traffick the children to the Monster. We knew. We all knew. So did her family. They knew everything, and they didn't care. And at this point I'd also like to thank Jackie, an old friend of

Devil's who knew and did nothing. She told Mick she thought about it, but didn't. Why? Why would you let little girls be hurt in this way? You are a big grown woman. Why would you let a child be hurt in this way. She parted friendship with Devil. Monster wanted it that way. So we decided to meet with the FBI. We went back to my son's house in Kankakee to meet them. They came right on time. Mary Jane and Buck. They asked us questions at first. We showed them pictures of the girls, and told them a bit about the girls. They were amazed. Buck didn't talk much. He was the listener. Mary Jane spoke. She said they were "in grave danger, and we needed to get them out of there." She also said that they needed to get Devil, Monster and Shorn's computers and investigate their computers. They would get those right away. And they wanted my son Mick, the girls Daddy to take a lie detector test, which he agreed immediately to do.

While they were there, the Kankakee police came. They had Devil's b.s. order of protection to serve on him. While the police came in Mary Jane and Buck hid in the girls bedroom. Which seemed so silly. Their car was in the driveway. When they left, we gave them all of our information. We had spoken for probably two hours. We actually felt hopeful. We actually felt someone cared. Oddly I had also received an email from a man who has a political conscience website, who told me that an "FBI" person was evaluating my case, was very interested and would be in touch with me. Don't know who that was, or if it ever happened. It was all very odd. The next day I awoke to a phone call. It was Buck. He wanted to return my notebook. Alright. He'd copied it and wanted to return it. I work the 3pm to 11 pm shift, so I was tired. But I got up and retrieved the book from him.

Then I heard nothing more. I know my son and Jess had some phone calls and conversation. I did not. Basically, they faded away. Buck started making excuses for the sex offender. Then he told them that he worked with Ernie Thomson and couldn't do anything to help us. Then he said that Emily's injury was only about an inch long, so it wasn't rape. Well a little girls space between her vagina and her rectum, is only about an inch long. I don't imagine a grown woman's is much more. And it was torn back to her rectum. And

116

she told her story. And she named her attacker. But they were done. Oddly, thereafter, possibly a month or so, my son and Jess were asked to meet with the FBI. My son and Jess lived in North Carolina. They came back to meet with Emmy, the superior, Mary Jane and Buck. They were told that they mostly wanted to talk to me, and chastise me for being on the computer and searching for help. I had gone to a website, and asked for help. Asking if anyone knew where my granddaughters were, that they were not to be with Monster, that there was a court order he could not have any contact, nor live with the children. And that the children told us he killed Martha. In a house fire. They were there. As a very strange aside, the girls named one woman who raped them, and her name was......"Emmy". Emmy explained that I was a problem. I was causing problems for them. What? I'm telling the truth, I'm asking for help, this man is trafficking these children (I knew Devil was with him, where else would she go with three kids?), and we needed help. And I'm a grown woman. I can put whatever I want onto my computer. This is America. There is free speech. The FBI in Champaign is more interested in me speaking the truth, than stopping a sex offender. And I'm crazy? Mick was appalled. He couldn't believe it. We had three little girls being trafficked by a sex offender, and their mother, and no one cared. They more cared about my outing the sex offender.

Where to turn? Where to turn?

I had gone to locals, police, DCFS, hospitals, lawyers, congressmen, senators, governors, doctors, FBI, and no one cared. No one cares about little girls being trafficked by a sex offender. This is appalling to me. Appalling. I have talked to so many victims of child sexual assault, and they all tell me the same thing. No one cares. No one helps. No one comes forward. And I believe them. Because I've been there. No one will help. I actually got a phone call from someone, I honestly don't remember who it was, who suggested that I call the DCFS in Kankakee. I said "No, don't do that, they don't help, they just do favors for the mother. We have presented them with everything, and they stopped their own investigation and gave the children back to the mother." This man told me "I'm calling them", and he hung up and he called. This investigation was going on during our final days of the court case, April 29, 2009, and they just mutilated us. The girls had to go in when Ernie Thomson was there. I remember how he smiled at us. I can't imagine the fear they felt. They knew they'd better not tell, or there would be severe consequences. I still cannot take it all in. It's a mess that has no resolve. It's a mess that we don't even know where to start to fix. Where do you go? Who do you call? The first thing you'd need would be a satchel full of cash for a huge attorney, and all the money would be sucked up immediately. Little girls don't matter. What's right doesn't matter. This will sound really harsh and I don't mean any personal charge against anyone specific, but it really irks me. We wonder about the reality of our society and the failings in this country. The challenged we face. The fall of greatness. No good jobs. Monies being lost. Well I guess we should care about the real things. Children. Old people. Justice. Doing the right thing. A society that does not take care of the old the young and the infirm....shall perish. What are we doing? What in the hell is happening? Why is this allowed? No child should face this hell.

I will never forget the oddest of ironies that day. As we left we learned that the courthouse at dusk would be the sight of a candle lighting ceremony. Candles lit for the survivors and victims of sexual assault. That day. Are you kidding me? I understand people's hopes for this horror to go away. But hands around the courthouse won't do it. Someone inside the courthouse, in the system, part of the good ole boys network will have to step in, and stop this hell upon children. Upon women as well. I understand people's hopes that it is going away. It's not going away. Til the judges send sex offenders to jail, til the mothers stop turning their children over to their sex offender boyfriends. Til someone has the balls to step up and stop this hell, no candles will do a thing. I applaud the efforts, but the judges, the courts, the police, the gendarmes are to blame. They need to be held accountable for the horror they place children in.

We saw nothing but favors done for a sex offender. Sick. Depraved. Large men, carrying guns, wearing badges, doing the dirty work for the sex offender. Monster.

118

Mick,

Girls and I stopped by to see ya, & they wanted to let you know they want to come tomorrow. I will drop them off around 10:30. If that doesn't work you need to let me know. Get your phone fixed, they miss talking to ya!!

Devil, Layla, Emily and Annie

And a few months later, this lying Devil, gets a two year order of protection that the father cannot see the children for two years. Two years.

Yes there is a Devil.

# Chapter 12 - Truth be Told

I have to speak for myself at this point. I have been drug through the mud like some sort of dirty dog. Devil lied so much that its hard to know if she ever tells the truth. The old joke....how can you tell if she's lying? Her lips are moving.

She actually got on the stand at one point and told the court that our family was ignorant, and had no education. That we were liars, and couldn't be trusted. She didn't want the children anywhere near us. (And that included our granddaughter Candi, who at the time was 7. And loved the girls. They were crazy about each other.) Although we watched the girls all the time. It was better sounding when you want to create a case against their father.

My husband Joe was third in his high school class. A straight A student. He graduated from the University of Illinois with honors. He became partners with a friend early in the seventies, of a chocolate factory. His partner had been in the dairy business. He wanted to do something that would impact the private label business, which was then coming to the fore. So they had a scientist develop a private label hot cocoa, and they sold it to grocery store chains. They had all of the large grocery store chains in the country. So much so, that in the late seventies my husband and I moved to California to service the west coast accounts from the west coast. West coast customers were unhappy when they had promotional sales going on, and their product was stuck in the Rockies!

After that venture, which he was involved in for about ten years, we moved back to Illinois. My husband and another friend started a ginseng farm. The friend had studied ginseng and felt that it was a crop that could bring a large harvest, and he had property that was perfect for this venture. However it was a seven year harvest, and involved a lot of work. All of it manual labor. The "beds" had to be raised and grown in the shade. My husband became the working partner and they were involved in the ginseng business for over fifteen years. I am very proud of the ginseng farm. All of my children at different times labored through the summer on the ginseng farm. My oldest son worked there after high school for awhile.

My husband was raised on a farm, and his grandfather was a very big farmer when he was a kid. So he respects the land and the value of hard work.

I was a manicurist. I worked in California while we lived there for a time. When we moved back to Illinois I started the first nail salon in the Kankakee area, and we were very fortunate to be very busy and have a lovely clientele. I had four different manicurists who worked with me, and I felt we were very successful. I remember being very busy.

I went back to school several years ago to become a certified nursing assistant. I now work as a cna at the local nursing home. It is a lovely place. It is fresh and clean and inviting. The residents are lovely people that I adore. I love my job. I love my co-workers. I love making people feel good about themselves. I wouldn't hurt a fly.

Devil tried to tell the court that we were some sort of indigent, ignorant people who had no life experience. We were some sort of idiots.

I am quite proud of my life experience. I have met and known some really wonderful people. I have had a great life.

I have raised three sons. I have four beautiful granddaughters. I have never harmed or desecrated my children nor my grandchildren, or any other child. Children are treated like the treasures that they are.

I love my life. I love my home. I live in a home that is over one hundred years old. I love it. I am not a person who brags about my bank account or my car. I am who I am.

I am a certified nursing assistant and almost sixty years old. My husband is sixty two and retired. He collects social security. He worked hard to get to this time of his life. He collects old bicycles and restores them. It is a hobby, but truly is a love. He loves the history and the life of old bicycles. And he has met many others who feel the same way.

My love is my family, and my home, and my friends. Our life is simple.

I do not try to impress anyone with anything I have. My life is just my life. My greatest treasures are the people in my life.

Devil trying to paint us as monsters is more a commentary on who she is, than on who we are. She does not know us. She knows nothing of me. She is a dark, evil, cold person. I do not know what her values are. Although when I did know her, her values seemed to be money and things. She loved nice cars, nice purses, and money. I guess she'd found her niche.

And she's evil. We received two copies of the court order regarding Monster not being with the children, that was basically a document made by the court to protect the children. On one which we received on 7-3-10, it stated "You people are all psychotic. Stick this crap up your ass! I hope you all burn in hell!" And on 7-19-10, "Hit's in Watch your back."

This document was designed to keep a sex offender from his victims.

My son tried to call the state police to tell them we had received death threats on the order of protection. He was told if he ever called again he would be arrested.

I believe she sent these to me as a warning. I had seen many people on their facebook accounts with little children. I had sent them a copy of the court order, and a letter that Dr. Judy wrote, regarding the lack of safety for the children in being near the Monster. I actually thought someone would care. One of their friends who was a nurse, who had small children, emailed me back and said "don't ever contact me again, if you do I will contact the police." I said "Go right ahead."

It is also amazing to know that when the judge was told that Devil was a liar, and had lied throughout the case, that the judge left the case, instead of calling her back and charging her with perjury. Remember Mark Fuhrman? Perjury? The case is stopped dead in its tracks and the perjurer is brought forward to be named a perjurer. And that is totally relevant. Not for my girls. Not for my girls.

More hell to come. Devil is the worst thing that has ever happened to our family. The worst.

# Chapter 13 - When the Truth is Found to be Lies

After the court date, and the FBI and all of the ridiculous insanity that took place, we were shell shocked. To say we had been left alone, left in hell, confused, shocked, lost, broken, was an understatement. I felt like I had been run over by an end loader, and then for good measure, they backed over me again.

I know my son felt the same way. All of us were heartbroken. The judge was so ignorant. She didn't listen. There would be one or two hours, and then she'd stop, and schedule another court hearing two or three months later. And often our attorney would show up from Chicago, only to find the court date had been changed, and no one notified him. I remember my son's lawyer writing a letter to the parties involved, and asking that at the least that he be made known of any changes. With these lapsed court dates, my son of course was still charged at the top Chicago lawyer prices. I know he spent so much money, and nothing ever materialized.

The Chicago lawyer left the case after the April 29, 2009 court date, and advised my son to never go there again, for fear of his life. The things that had happened in that courthouse were not right. The lawyer claimed he would not come back. He had never seen anything like the gendarmes charging us out of the courthouse. The intimidation was just unreal.

The mother always won. She always made sure that the children were with the sex offender.

I was really so hurt and broken. I know my son was too. We all were. Dealing with the pain and loss and confusion was such a hurdle. Until that time, we had seen the girls every week, sometimes for several days at a time. We missed them terribly and feared for them even more. We knew where they were. We absolutely knew where they were. And the agony of what was happening to them was just so close to our conscience. We knew why Monster trafficked them out of state. So he could abuse them. That's what sex offenders, pedophiles do. They hurt children.

Probably almost a year later, I spent time on the computer searching for them. I always felt that there was some way or some how that I could and would find them. One night I paid for a search on an internet site that finds people. I forget what I paid. Possibly eighty dollars or so. It printed out several minutes later in my email account. I looked at it and found that Monster Thomson indeed lived in Conroe, Texas. I looked it over several times. In the possible contacts was Devil Mazur. I looked at that a few times, before it finally hit me. She was living with him at the same address. Bingo. I'd found them.

I waited a few days, unsure of what to do. I know we had contacted the FBI who did nothing. Told us we had to go through Texas. Well the court order that he could have no contact was issued in Illinois. Illinois said it was Texas' problem. Texas said it was Illinois'' problem. Pretty convenient, as no one has to do their job. Let little girls be raped.

So after awhile, I called the police in Texas. I was put in touch with a Deputy Glissen with child welfare. He indeed went out to the location to speak with the landlord. Indeed, he was shown the lease, which had all five of them on the lease. Monster, Devil, and the children. She had defied the court order. She had lied to the courts, again. She had taken the children straight to Texas, and placed them with the sex offender, against court orders. This is called child trafficking. Taking children across state lines to place them with a sex offender, who is to have no contact. Child trafficking.

The police in Texas, we were told did an investigation into the situation with their division of DCFS. Which was ridiculous. The children were not allowed to tell the truth. They knew that. And Monster and Devil had already violated the court order of having no contact, and not living with the sex offender. Illinois should have ordered them back in front of the judge.

Instead, the judge left the case. She said that it was an "exparte communication which directly impacted the credibility of the witnesses at the hearing on the petition to remove". In other words, the mother and her witnesses lied on their reasons for moving the children. She trafficked the children to the sex offender. Unbelievable. Unbelievable. And her witnesses lied for her. Just unbelievably wicked and disgusting.

I went to the courthouse, to ask for a copy of the order that Monster could have no contact with the children. I wanted to send it to Texas. The clerk told me the file was not able to be found. The entire file of the case of the children and court was gone. Where was it? She fumbled about for awhile, and finally told me that Judge A had taken it on her vacation. What? She took it on vacation. What if she was killed or her house burned down and the file was lost? Why did she take it home?

I went to talk to a court clerk. She was stunned by everything. She simply looked me in the eyes, and said very clearly "Get this in front of a judge now, like yesterday. They are violating the order."

My son didn't know what to do. He went to a local attorney, the first he had hired, and had fired, and she agreed to take it on. She said she would take care of everything. He gave her the retainer fee, and believed she would do her job. I'm not sure now, after the fact, why he did this, but we were all so broken and twisted, its not hard to see that none of us really knew what to do. We actually felt that once it was shown that the mother trafficked the children across state lines to victimize them, that the entire ball would come rolling down, and the insanity would stop. Finally.

How wrong we were. The next rift of insanity had begun.

The case languished. My son kept calling the lawyer and asking her if she had filed an emergency order. She assured him that she had. Nothing was done. The court dates kept getting backed up and backed up. My son was lost. We were lost. He had spent all of the money he had left to acquire this attorney, so we were now really in the pits of hell. She did nothing.

The case was continued, and continued and continued. I believe it took six months before it ever went in front of a new judge.

We finally went before the new judge, Judge K. What a moron this guy was. He had no insight into the case, and obviously had read nothing. He was only interested in Devil's claim that she hadn't received all her child support. This had already been decided by the first judge, and the payments came steadily. She advised that she had been paid nothing, again, all the while we had many many receipts. Then she was allowed to cherry pick which receipts she claimed were real. She had done nothing but lie, and traffick her children, and she was the person whom the judge believed. My son was treated like dirt. He had facebook with the fact that she was living with the sex offender against court order, he had proof that she was engaged and soon to marry the sex offender, he had all these horrible comments that were made by the sex offender regarding the father. I later went to a meeting with an FBI agent who handles cases of child sexual offenders. She informed us that courts and judges indeed use facebook and any communication to show that someone is with children and molesting children. She was dumbfounded by what I told her. She told me to send all the information, and like everyone else, did nothing.

My son had proof that the sex offender and the mother had trafficked the children all over the globe. They had traveled to Texas, Florida, Illinois, Oklahoma, Hawaii, and Brazil. Yes Brazil. He had trafficked the girls out of the country at a time when he was court ordered to have no contact. And no one cared. No one would lift a finger to stop them. And this was in their own words on their facebook accounts.

We knew the children had gone to Florida and were trafficked by the sex offender within seven months of the time the court order was written. The girls came home from Florida, and were on my front porch. My son had given Devil a thousand dollars to spend on the girls on vacation. As they sat on my front porch I asked them about vacation. The twins were oddly quiet. Annie started chatting about swimming in Bonnie's pool and staying at her house. I said innocently "who's Bonnie?" Annie, not realizing anything said "that's Monster's Mom"....I said "where was Monster?" She said "he was there too, we stayed there." What? He is to have no contact, and you are in Florida with him. Amazing. And Eliza, aka Rocksy went with them too. So the friends are working with the sex offender to have his victims as well. Later on Emily told me that Monster put his penis in her in Florida. And Devil made reference to being in Brazil with the sex offender and the children on her facebook account. Have I died and gone to hell?

All of Devil's friends were just joking and laughing on their facebook account. "So happy about your engagement, congratulations on your engagement,"......and he's not even supposed to be with the children. He lives with them, he vacations with them, and the mother is engaged to him.

And the FBI couldn't find this? The police couldn't find this? I found it. Rather easily once I started poking my nose into things. I thought that is what the police and FBI did. I thought they poked their nose into the business of a sex offender who was trafficking little children all across the globe against court order. I was wrong.

We felt that the story of the girls being trafficked to Texas, amongst other places would indeed be told. Never mentioned. Never brought up. In fact when the court date to discuss my son seeing his children finally came up, my son's lawyer told my son to let his girlfriend Jess take the stand. She would be questioned as to her viability to be a chaperone if there could be a visitation with the girls. (Never mind that the girls were in Texas, alone with the sex offender at the time this was taking place. Insanity.) And it was also the girls birthday. The twins were seven I believe. My son was praying he would see them after two long years apart.

No. Not to be. Devil's lawyer had five or six pages of questions for Jess on legal paper. Why did my son's lawyer suggest this line of questioning? For the opposition? How odd. Crazy. Insane.

My son just had a horrible time during that hearing. It was insane. He was about to burst. The mother on the stand telling that she was so fearful of the father, and didn't want him to see the children, and the children were living with the sex offender in Texas against court order. Unbelievable. Just insane.

So as we languished knowing all of this, waiting to get it in front of the judge, the monster kept raping the girls. My son actually received a phone call from Monster telling him he'd better back off, or Monster would come to Illinois and blow me and my son away with a shotgun. That these girls were his, and he would do whatever he wanted to do with them. He would rape them, and beat them, and do whatever he wanted. When they got home from school he would do whatever he wanted to do. He called my son twice. We have the records of those phone calls.

Again, no one did anything. I called DCFS in Texas to tell them what happened and asked them to check on the girls to see if they were safe. Well we knew they weren't safe, they were with a pedophile. I called the police and was told I had to call DCFS. I was on hold on the phone for an hour. When I finally reached them they assured me they would check on the girls. The next day my husband said to me, "Call them back and find out what was done." I called and was told that there was a notation on the file "this was addressed in a previous incident, nothing done." What? A previous incident. I had never called before. There was never a previous incident. More of the lazies doing nothing. No one gave a damn and no one did their job.

Devil and Monster could do whatever they wanted, whenever they wanted, and leave every bit of evidence, and no one gave a damn. No one did a thing. Little girls left in hell.

When we finally did get back into court it was the twins birthday. The mother Devil was there. She got on the stand with a card that she said I had sent that was a threat. I never sent her anything. And she said it was mailed to Monster Ernie sex offender. Why would she have Monster Thomson's mail? Because she lived with him against court order. Anyway, she was allowed to show a card and say I sent it with no proof, and the judge accepted that. My son was not allowed to show anything. No facebook with their words, their intentions, their lives. But she could say and do whatever she wanted. She said the children were wonderful and didn't ever ask about their father. Sure. She then cherry picked the receipts that she had signed, and was allowed to do so.

My son was sitting at the desk, totally confused and beaten. When Devil yells to her lawyer "Jeff, he just said he's going to kill me." My son says "Here we go again." He'd never said that. Never. So as my son left court, he was arrested and placed in jail. On the fourth of July weekend. On the weekend of his daughters' birthday. As we left the courthouse, Jess was stunned. As was I and my husband. Devil and her mother drove their car on the street we were parked on, and slowed and stopped to take in their satisfaction at what they'd done. More lies from the liar. God she was good.

She could say and do anything and she was believed. All the while she was trafficking her children about the globe against court order with a sex offender. Brilliant. Brilliant. Except for the fact that she was destroying the lives of three little girls.

This was just unbelievable.

My son had to wait several months for the court date. He had to eventually wear a bracelet on his ankle so that the police could monitor his whereabouts as he was a threat to Devil. Remember she always had a court order that he could not come near her or threaten her, and supposedly he had threatened her in the courtroom.

So he had to move back to Illinois from his girlfriend's in North Carolina. He had to wear a bracelet on his ankle, which was a mess. It always ran out of juice, it was defective. Everytime it would run out of juice, the police would call to see where he was. If he wasn't where he was supposed to be, then they could arrest him immediately. I believe he wore it in excess of a month. And had to pay for the privilege of wearing it!

And when the court date came for her to have him prosecuted for his threat......she didn't show up. Didn't even show up. She had only done this to threaten him, and have her last grand stand to beat him up. She was really a showman. Really laying it down.

We in fact got the transcript of the court case. My son said nothing to her. Not a word. But her word, the word of a liar, was always listened to and believed. Unbelievable. Just disgusting.

We also had the letter from the court appointed, let me repeat that....court appointed psychologist that stated "On 4-09-10 Monster Thomson left a voice mail on my office phone in Champaign, Illinois. Monster said he lives with Devil and "the three girls" stating, "I take care of his kids...send them to school, to the doctor." Monster said that Mick is sending the letter I had written concerning him (Monster) to Monster's friends and family in which Monster stated, "I continue to be abused by him."

Monster is abused by my son. Monster is abused by my son. What a crock. This guy is just the end of the f#$ing world isn't he? He's raping little girls, and he's being abused! What a nut case. What a nut job.

Monster Thomson admitting to the court appointed psychologist that he has the children, against court order. Trafficking the children.

I, not Mick, had sent the letter Dr. Judy wrote to friends of Monster and Devil as I feared he would hurt more of the children of their friends. The girls had told of us other children being part of being hurt. The letter stated in part "Without Mr. Thomson's completion of a psychosexual evaluation by a expert with a report provided to the Court, the three children, Layla, Emily and Annie would need to be considered at high risk of harm in his presence.

I guess at this point, I am speechless. This case had rendered me speechless many many times. The nuts are running the asylum. If this is where we are in cases of sexual assault at this time in America, then dear God, we are in deep trouble.

I always thought the people who ran the system were intelligent people who had empathy for others. Especially for little girls who were at the hands of a Monster. But I have not met that person yet.

I really think its time for this country to take a very serious look at this problem and make some real changes. No little girl should have to live what my granddaughters are living......ever......

And when my son went back to court for the final evaluation by Judge K, who frankly didn't know his ass from a whole in the ground, he decided that my son had paid nothing, and ordered him to pay $30,000 in back support.

This was a lie. A total untruth. My son was to pay the mother who trafficked her children to a violent sex offender in spades. And none of his receipts to her for the past several years were applied to the debt.

It is amazing to know that this is what we experienced in a courthouse in America. Amazing.

----

132

# Chapter 14 - Silence of the lambs

Devil Devil, to me, is a Monster, as well as Monster Thomson. They live by torturing and hurting others. Little ones mostly. I saw Devil do this in many ways to many people. But one of the ugliest incidents came in the way of my mother, who is now in her eighties.

My mother has worked her entire life. She struggled through some pretty crappy low paying jobs, then went on to work in a factory in the seventies where she made decent money, but had long hard hours. She finally became a licensed practical nurse in her sixties, and worked in that field for many many years. My mother in fact paid for Devil's wedding gown when she didn't have enough money to pay for it, and always helped them whenever and however she could.

She has had a few health scares, the most recent, walking her dog, and being attacked by a neighbor dog, which took her to the ground and broke her hip. A serious injury for an elderly woman.

My mother is not one to ask for sympathy or special needs. She goes on about her life and does what needs to be done. My mother has always been a person who believes in another's civil rights. Something I learned about as a child.

She lives in Kankakee which has a generous population of diversity. One night she was going to work (she worked the night shift) and she saw two police officers manhandling a black man. They were hitting him and clubbing him, and forcing him into the back seat of their squad car. She stopped (she'd do this on many occasions) and yelled at them "Stop hitting that man, you're going to hurt him." They yelled at her to keep driving. She stopped her car, and got out and demanded their names and badge numbers.

The next day she called their sergeant who told her to mind her own business, and leave the police alone. She of course, told him what she thought of him. And that civil rights was her business.

One day my mother was going to her favorite furniture store of thirty years, that happens to be across the street from Devil's mother's house. She could hear someone laughing at her and saying her name. She looked across the street to Devil and Rocksy laughing at her. They were really quite tickled with themselves.

My mother, being my mother, turned with her walker, and walked across the street. She pointed at Devil and told her she ought to be ashamed of herself, and what she was allowing to happen to her children, and that one day she would pay for what she had done.

She turned and left, with them giggling and laughing at her.

Another time, my mother met my son at the courthouse, to be a show of support. So many court dates. She was very disgusted with what she saw, as we all always were. The judge was very accommodating to the Devil and her family and always very short with my son. When my mother left the courthouse, she was talking to my son, telling him how disgusted she was, and what a joke that courtroom was. Which, quite seriously, it was.

Police officers followed my mother, and told her she couldn't say anything bad about a judge, and she had to leave.

Is this America? Don't we have free speech. Can't you say that a judge is bad, and you don't like her? No, you may not. And as it turns out, my mother was the only one in that courthouse that said what was true. The judge was abhorrent, and Devil was a liar. So, indeed she was right. And history showed us that the judge was wrong, wrong, wrong.

As an aside, I went to a later court date, and was told the maternal grandmother could not be in the court room. That she had done something wrong. The police officer in the courtroom brought this to the attention of the judge. That mattered to the judge. That someone disagreed with her. Not that three little girls were being trafficked all over the globe. My mother indeed was the maternal great grandmother, but rather than cause any turbulence for the judge I got up and left. God forbid someone didn't like her, while she's allowing three little girls to live in hell.

This is a part of my life that I have quite seriously been very afraid for people in this country. When little girls can't get anyone to listen when they are being brutalized, something is very wrong. And as I read about this subject and see programs about this subject, I learn that Devil is not alone. There are many many women who think it is alright to trade your child or children for a man who pays your bills, keeps you, and provides for you, and rapes your kids.

My mother, like myself, and many others I know, is dumbfounded that our society, full of men and women who have made many sacrifices for this country, are ignored when it comes time for the system to step in and do the right thing.

This will always be my calling as I move forward. When someone in a position of power knows that little children need help, they will pitch in and make it stop. Not just pass it along, and pass it along.

Like I've always said, I fear one of my granddaughters will be dead or terribly injured before this Monster is stopped. These monsters, I should say. These Monsters. Any mother who whores out her own children to keep a man for herself, is just a Monster.

# Chapter 15 - The Baby Stroller

I'm not sure if its appropriate but its yelling at me in my conscience, so I feel I should finish what I started.

The most glaring of events that truly alerted me to the vicious nature of Devil and her mother Shorn, were the events regarding Devil's pregnancies.

She was pregnant twice and miscarried. She got pregnant before the wedding. They wed and she became pregnant again, and miscarried. On the third try, I prayed, we all did, that she would carry the baby to term.

As time went on and she got to the sixth, seventh, eighth month, I thought we had finally arrived at success and a baby would come into their lives. We were ecstatic. It was a little boy. My son had arrived on the name Boston, as he and his father, are huge Red Sox fans. My son was just so excited. He was counting the days until his little boy would be in his arms.

I'll never forget the pain of waking up on July 2, 2000. I was sound asleep in bed. I heard a voice say "Mom", and I knew something was very wrong. My son was sitting in my chair in my bedroom. He said "They think the baby's dead." I said "What?" He repeated it. "the baby's dead."

I said "How can that be, she's in her eighth month."

I got up and I ran to my husband, who was downstairs, and told him, "We're going to the hospital, the baby is dead."

My son and Devil then lived in Kankakee, which was forty minutes away. We drove very quickly. I kept trying to convince myself, that he had misunderstood, or something else happened. I just couldn't begin to comprehend that his baby was dead.

When we got to the hospital, he had a dead bird hanging in the grill of his Jeep, very similar to the movie, *Silence of the Lambs*, when the guard is hanging on the cell. My son and I immediately felt that it was a very bad sign. And it was.

We went into the hospital and indeed the baby was dead. The mother was in her eighth month. She had a week previously, after suffering two miscarriages, went to her mother's to pick up a baby stroller.

In her eight month. Her mother Shorn, hadn't brought it to the shower because it was too heavy for her to carry. Never mind that we had several men at the shower who carried everything in and out for us. She left it at home. So Devil went to pick it up the next week. My son at the time traveled out of town all week for work. So he was not at home. As I was told, her mother wanted it "out of her house, it was in the way." So Mother, eight months pregnant, went to her mother's to pick up the offending stroller.

Now keep in mind, that I had previously seen Shorn's driveway. It was a nightmare. I was afraid to walk on it, as a regular person. It was broken into a thousand pieces that were at all different levels, and was just a disaster waiting to happen. Unbelievably dangerous. A broken ankle, a broken leg, or in our case, a dead baby.

Devil drug the big box down the driveway as best she could, and was pulling so hard, that she fell backwards and fell on her butt. She fell with such force, that she went into labor.

She went to the hospital, and they stopped her labor, and sent her home. They never checked the placenta. Which had actually torn, and the baby was inside her with no life support.

All for a stupid baby stroller. That Shorn couldn't bring to the shower because it was too big, but her eight month pregnant daughter could pick it up.

Have I lost my mind?

These people did things that just made your brain explode. Who does that? My parents didn't let me pick up anything when I was pregnant. Nothing. A stroller box, down a dangerous driveway at eight months! Come on.

My son was devastated. I believe Devil was too, but refused to show it.

At the funeral home, after the service, I was up and ready to walk out of the service area. I noticed my husband going back to my son who was standing at the coffin of his baby. Devil at the time was standing by the front door, looking agitated as he was taking too long. He wanted to say good bye to his son, and ask God why this had to happen.

But we learned very quickly there would be no conversation about why or anything else, as it was offending Devil and Shorn. My son could not grieve or have anyone talk to him about his pain, because it made Devil and Shorn upset. How about the pain he was in at the loss of his baby.

For Shorn and Devil the subject was closed. No conversation. In fact, my son wanted to take a match and some lighter fluid to the stroller and burn it because he was so pained looking at the damn thing. No, couldn't be done. Might upset Shorn. She bought it!

So my husband and I went back and talked and cried with my son. He couldn't leave his son. He couldn't bear walking away. He needed a moment to try and understand or say goodbye.

He turned to his father and me and said "All I can keep thinking is "You can't always get what you want." And shook his head.

I said "We will never know why honey, but we will always have him in our hearts and love him forever."

We all walked out together, arm in arm, tears flowing.

Devil marched out like "finally".

138

When we got to the cemetery, it was a beautiful day. Just gorgeous. Every person there loved Mick and his wife at the time. Their faces were just agony. The pain they felt for them was just like a painted scenery in a play.

The car doors of the black limousine opened, and Mick went to the back door, and took out his little baby boy in his casket, which to me looked like a beer cooler, and really upset me. But I was told that is what baby's are buried in.

My son walking with his baby, with what looked like the weight of the world on his shoulders, was so heartbreaking, and heart warming all at once. This little boy was wanted and loved and Daddy was taking him to his final resting spot.

In that moment, TJ came from nowhere in jeans, and threw his arm over Mick's and was more of a burden to my son than a help. I just wanted to rewind, and have my son doing what he was doing for his son.

What heartbreak this was. Tragedy. Just tragic.

I later talked to a woman who had her nails done at the salon where Devil was working as a cleaning lady. She went on and on about this woman who smoked like a fiend, always had a cigarette in her mouth, pregnant and smoking like a fiend, and laughing about it.

I asked her what the girls name was. It was indeed Devil.

My heart broke. Such sadness. I just couldn't reconcile her behavior with anything I'd ever known. Every pregnant Mommy I ever knew was so careful throughout her pregnancy to be so careful. I was heartbroken.

Amazingly, I had a psychic on a website, shortly after Boston's birth, tell me, that Boston was a twin spirit. He went back to heaven so he could come back in life with his twin spirit. It would either be two girls or two boys. They would come in the same cycle. It would be two years apart. And they would be identical, except one would have something that would show that Boston was there. There would be a marking on one of them that would be different.

The twins came two years after Boston. They were born on July 3, 2002. They are identical except for a marking on Layla's eye. Layla will show that marking and tell people, that is my baby brother Boston.

Amazing.

I had tried on a few occasions to talk to Shorn about Boston. Just grandmother to grandmother about the pain we experienced, about the pain the children were in, how I was so hopeful for a baby to come for Mick and Devil. She would become enraged and tell me to shut up.

I realize people will think I am being unfair in my characterization, but I know no one who would have acted in any way as Shorn and Devil did throughout this first lost pregnancy, nor what has happened to the children.

They just aren't right. Something is terribly wrong.

# Chapter 16 - From The Mouths of Babes

I feel it is so necessary for me to tell this story in the girls words. As best I feel that I can. The twins were six and the baby was four. They had asked us repeatedly if they could speak to someone, anyone who might help them. They were well aware that they were in danger and needed help. Little girls who are gang raped and tortured know its wrong. They know it. Their Mother Devil's family wouldn't help them. That they knew. They also knew that they were not allowed to speak the truth with the Devil's family. That was well ingrained in them. by Monster, by Devil, by Shorn, by Sorry, by everyone in Devil's court. (Remember in Dr. Judy's report Mommy saying to them when they would speak of being hurt "do you want me to cut off all of your hair.") Talk about brutal. But they also knew that we would listen, and we would try to help them. So they always asked, and always pleaded with us to help them. Can you imagine being a captive in your Mother's camp, which is a camp of lies, pain, torture, hell, rape, child trafficking? ( I worried about silly things at age six.) Little girls, captive in hell. The Devil is their captor. I can hear Annie's actual voice, and I hear it often, when she turned to me one day, out of nowhere, at age 3 "Mommy's with the Devil." I will never forget it. It will never leave me. She was simply playing, and something she was playing with gave her a thought, or a moment, and she turned to me, and simply said it clear as a bell. "Mommy's with the Devil." Amen.

Just before the last court date, the girls stayed with their father for ten days while their mother went away on a trip. (Remember after the mother got home, less than a week later, after voluntarily leaving the girls with their father, while she was on her trip, she wrote up her bullshit order of protection for two years!) So very fearful is she, that she left the girls alone with him......The girls knew when they were left with their father,  that their mother Devil, and Monster had gone "somewhere". They did not know where, but knew that Devil and Monster had gone to look for a place to live. They were going to this place whether they won the last court case or not. The girls were very fearful of being moved away, not seeing their Daddy, and living with Monster. Their stories were so very heightened and scarey. The incidents of sexual assault, and the gravity of the assaults had heightened, and they were terrified. More and more people were assaulting them, and it was becoming more frequent. They did not want to leave their father. They were afraid. And they listened in enough to Monster and Devil's conversations, to know that they were indeed moving, and they were not to tell us. They tried so hard to figure out where, and when and tell us, but couldn't seem to find that out. They were so darling in trying to fight for themselves. I remember my sick sadness, when Layla told me that she thought she had a semen soaked Kleenex (dirty rag she called it with Monster's stuff on it), but told me her mother saw it in her pocket, on visitation day, and took it away from her. Layla thought if she showed me that, I could show it to the police, or the judge and they could see it was Monster's stuff and tell him to stop. Now I ask you, are there any of you reading this, that can even handle the image that has flooded your brain? (I had many of these horrific conversations that tore out my heart and my brain with the girls. They were so smart, and tried so hard. It's just abysmal that any little girl has this horror in her daily life.) I'd burst into tears at the drop of a hat, when I'd be thinking of the girls, and one of these horrors would cross my mind. Horrors. Horrors.

The girls had asked their Dad repeatedly if they could talk to the judge. Mick had told the girls earlier, that Mommy and Daddy were talking to a judge, and she was going to help the girls with their problems. This was when we still actually believed that someone would care, and help them. The girls wanted to tell the judge how scary being with Monster was, and that they needed help. They would often ask their father, and me "Does the judge know? Did you get to tell her? Will she help us?" The girls would come for visitation, after a particularly really bad week, and beg us "when will the judge help us? Doesn't she care?"

Trying to tell the children that the judge didn't care, and that actually, no one seemed to care, was nearly impossible. Remember, the judge had ordered that we could not talk to the

142

children about their mother or time with their mother. And all the girls wanted to tell us was that their mother left them with Monster. And that Monster hurt them.  And that Monster's friends hurt them.

We had been cuffed and silenced. It  was the most horrific feeling I could ever express to anyone.  And the girls would become angered. They would say "You said she would help us. Why doesn't she do something?"  We were in no man's land. Imagine that horror.......I actually remember Layla saying to me "You said if we told, someone would help us."  I said "You don't tell when you're with Devil, and she says we are liars."  Layla would place both of her arms to her sides, outstretched, and scream,  "Why don't they get it? Devil won't let us tell. She wants to marry Monster.   Monster hurts us!!!!"   And let's always remember, Martha was murdered in front of them. The messages are loud and clear.  And as a very interesting aside, the fire chief of the area Martha lived in, has now been terminated, is now under indictment   for  serious  wrongdoing  in  the  fire  department. Hmmmmm.  More bad guys.

I feel I need to make this part crystal clear. The girls knew that what was being done to them was wrong, and that they needed an avenue, a place, a person, someone to tell. Someone who cared. Someone who would listen. This person could not be talking to them when they were with their Mother Devil or Devil's family, or Monster, because they made very serious scary threats to the girls. And the Devil's family was firmly entrenched in Monster's pocket. They would not hear of anything.  These little girls knew that they had no avenue to tell anyone. So telling this story was a big thing for them.  To see their hopes dashed was always very difficult.

We were so stupid in believing in the system, that we actually believed that possibly someone would see their plea for help.  Not to be.

So while their mother was with Monster, searching out her apartment to live with Monster, in Texas, (remember we weren't aware of where they were for almost a year) the girls asked their father on the final night, before Devil was to come home, could we please find a way to tell the judge what Monster does to them.

(There was no excitement that Devil was coming home. Only fear.) Knowing the judge would not speak to them, my son decided to speak to each girl and allow each of them to make their own plea themselves. Little girls, reaching out, to an unknown person, hoping, praying for help.

We also wanted the girls story to be recorded, as we actually feared, and still fear to this day, that they would totally disappear or leave the country. That would be for the sake of the sex offender. (Keep in mind, that the Devil, the Monster, Fern, TJ, Floyd, Shari, Rocksy, had all told lies to facilitate the sex offender being with the children.) And our greatest fear; that he may one day kill one of them. And we will receive the news that we have dreaded from day one. Still is our greatest fear.

So, the following is what we did, in the last hours before they left, on their last visit, before one of the last court dates: I took two girls for a walk, or we sat on the porch, while the other child solo told their plea of sadness. The girls were very ready to talk and tell their story. They'd asked us for this for over two years. It's very difficult for me to watch. I believe I've watched it once by myself. Once with the girls, as they asked me to, and once by myself. (I actually turned it on to see their little faces and hear their little voices.) I miss them desperately. The sadness is just deafening. That a judge didn't hear their sadness and see their pain.......Emily could barely tell her story. Trying to tell her story of fear and pain, made her recoil in visible pain. Such sadness. I cannot begin to tell you the pain and sadness we all felt, as a family. We knew, the girls knew, we all knew that the worst was yet to come. And there was no safety net. Flying without a net.

The judge, did not care. Did not care at all. She had watched it before the final court date before the mother trafficked the children to the sex offender. Told us at the last court date, that we made it up. Made it up. If you watch this dvd, your heart would break. A few of my very close friends who have watched it, have been totally heartbroken by it. Little girls don't say these things. Three little girls, let me repeat that..........little girls......trying to find the right words to say for someone to help them. For anyone to listen. It's just unfathomable.

144

Remember as you read this, that these are two twin girls who are six and a baby who is four. Speaking of being raped, by their Devil mother's boyfriend, Monster 96JD118, (who by the way, is a sex offender, court ordered to have no contact) terrifying and raping them. And of more people who come in, and rape them too. What children tell such stories? Out of thin air.

The girls had been playing with a package of silly little monsters, and they decided they wanted those to be their "people". They had talked to Daddy about the fact that it was time to tell their story to the judge. These would be their characters and they were ready. In fact, if it weren't such a hauntingly horrific story, it is almost endearing that these little girls, sought out the time, place, characters, and way that they would tell their story. Their story of hell. They acted out what they were saying. They knew their day of reckoning was coming. They were being taken away by the Monster. They knew that their time had come. They sat at our family room table, with their little monsters, and acted out their stories. It is so heartbreaking, that its deafening. It is basically a conversation between three little girls and their Daddy of being gang raped. Pleading for someone to help.........their final plea.

How many dashed hopes had they had? 1. Their initial plea to us on Teddy's birthday, 4/29/2007 2. their pleas to the Danville DCFS worker, 3. their plea to Dr. Kruzak when they suffered rape injuries, and were taken to the hospital, 4. their plea to their personal doctor, Dr. Ook, who let them sit for almost an hour, while he actually was waiting for Devil to pick them up, after they showed rape injuries, and were there for treatment, with paperwork from the head of the emergency room , 5. their plea to the KC CASA worker and the DCFS worker when they went to the hospital, 6. their pleas to their teachers, who never listened, 7. their many many tears and breakdowns at my home, 8. their pleas when they told us they had witnessed a murder and a fire, 9. their pleas to Dr. Judy, (in Dr. Judy's report, Devil says she'll cut off all their hair if they keep saying this), 10. Their plea to my friend Cyndi, their many pleas when they could really take no more...........who puts children through this hell? 11. This one is my personal favorite, of absolute insanity, and came after the sex offender and their Devil mother trafficked them to the sex offender in Texas. Dr. Judy reported to Judge A that Monster called her from Texas, and said "I have the children, I take care of them, take them to school, take them to the doctor," (A sex offender is taking the children to the doctor, and the Devil is working at a school!!! Against Illinois court order! Good God is there no sanity in this world! I guess they won't be telling the doctor, or showing their injuries! And a sex offender's girlfriend is working at an elementary school! And the sex offender has just proudly declared to the court appointed psychologist, that he is defying the court order, along with the Devil. Boastfully. ) An elementary school. And I mean, I could continue to reiterate hideous things like this over and over and over and over. Ad nauseum. You've read them. You know the truth. Everyone knows the truth. No one does anything to protect three little girls from a sex offender who is trafficking them sexually with the complete approval of their Devil mother.

Sex offender and Devil mother have taken children across state lines and national boundaries. Against court orders. News at 6:00.

And nothing is done......nothing........I guess instead of going to court, hiring lawyers, and fighting for the children, we all should have gone fishing. We would've at least had some fun and possibly caught dinner. And we could've all saved a lot of money. Mostly their Daddy. He spent so much money in the legal system. I know it had to be close to $50,00 to $60,000. And he finally found some lawyers in Chicago, who specialize in this type of case work. He went to them for a few consultations. They were stunned and blown away by the insanity that had gone on in this case, and continued to go on.

Because of the insanity, and the mess the case had become, and the fact that the children were now in Texas, their retainer would be $20,000. That would be just to open their door and open the file. To go to Texas and go after the Devil and the Monster, would of course, be more. Devil and Monster knew that by taking this hell to Texas, they had firmly placed us in a deep hole.

The lights are on, and nobody's home!

146

First to speak is Layla, the oldest twin, (by one minute):

Layla "This is Monster, and what's his name again? (Looks at her dad with a question on her face) Daddy says cautiously, not wanting to make her say something she doesn't want to say....."You mean Ernie", and she says as she remembers on her own, she says, "No Monster", (so if indeed Daddy was trying to coach her, she wasn't listening, and again who cares about the name, what about the details!), "and he comes in and he gets one of us and he does this with our chachi, and what is it called again....his penis, and he puts us back in and takes another one, and then this is well okay I'll tell you in a minute, this is me this is Emily and this is Annie and this is Monster's best.....his name is Mike....and his name is Earl, (holding up little dolls) and Monster's dad and Mom and Gramma, and his Mom, and this is a guy watching, his name is they usually call him Elly, and his name is Mikey, and this one is a person who is Mom and she comes down here to watch Mom going to sleep, and this is Elly.

"Where's Mommy?"

"Mom is here." (Motions to all of the figures who are gathered on the table)

Daddy speaks up " where is Mom in the house?"

Layla " So okay laying down right here, in the bed,"

Mick "And so where's Mommy sleep?"

Layla "Downstairs."

Mick "Whose house are you at?"

Layla "Gramma's. Mommy is there and all these people here." (Gestures to the figures on the table.)

Mick "You were saying you and the girls , Layla, where are you, where are you in the house?"

Layla "When he takes us he puts this guy over here, on the couch, and then um Monster comes over, and does what I showed you guys, (she takes a doll and gives us the visual, a doll and placing its penis area in another doll) and then he puts another one in and does it, and keeps on going, and then he has a cousin who does it too, and he's about three years old, and he still does it. But Annie though is shy, that's it." (They have often spoke of Annie's shyness, and that she cries throughout, which has always given me the shivers. It all does, but that just has always touched my heart.)

Mick "Is that it, is that all you want to say, What happens to these other people that are here, at Gramma Fern's, one more thing, where is Monster?"

Layla "And then he walks in and he says you know where Monster is, so he takes Monster, and he gets him and he talks to him. What? Then.... and then our dad punches him and punches everybody until they're all dead."

Mick "What's that. All the people are dead. When was Daddy there."

Layla "With a knife. Like Easter, he never got in my story, but like he got up again, and had this other guy, and Ernie came over and he had the girls, and he....."

Mick "When did this happen. Your dad came and got you and you ran out?"

Layla "you are like there, Monster did it before, and his friend is the Dad, and its like we don't know who it is for real, and then the story goes on,"

Mick " Wait, What does that mean, I'm getting lost, a friend comes over and knocks on the door, and pretends its your Dad? Where does the dad come in. Who is that guy?"

Layla " His name is not really Daddy, they usually call him that. He acts like the Dad, and knocks on the door, and, I'll pretend like this is real."

Mick " And where are you, do you ever, where's Mommy? How can Mommy not hear this."

Layla "They usually don't know, I told you everything, should probably be it, the end."

Mick "Okay, let me ask you this, Where do these people come here?"

Layla "They come here like every day. But they usually, Ernie parks his car in the garage, his siren gets caught, so he has to back it up, and like um, Monster's car is in the garage, and then he tries to back in and it's a car like Monster's car, he doesn't always have that car and usually he does take his own police car."

Mick "Why does he have a police car?

Layla " Cause he's a police. So they both try to park in the garage, and then he has to park in there, so there's no room and he parks this way. (motions sideways) Monster tries to get in and Ernie tries to get in. They park sideways. Ernie, all the cars in the back are, yea some people they bring their animals and they put them in a jar, and they like show us them and then we pass out." (Layla motions with an imaginary jar, in her hands and then places it up to her face, and pretends to pass out, and motions with her hand like, that's what happens)....author's note......this is drugging a child to incapacitate them for the purpose or raping them aka the Revlon heir, who is in jail. Jail.

Mick "what do you mean?"

Layla "so then the guy who acts like Dad goes over to say "What's the matter? And then he goes back to sleep......then its morning all the guys go home.....and they all come back."

Mick "Who's there, is anybody there? Where's Monster sleep?"

Layla " This is another story about him, and this is the one I saw, I got up early, because I wanted to watch and I went back in my room. So then I was back there in bed, and I was friends with her and Monster. And she acts these things out and she was kind of crazy and she has a van full of people and Shelly had some and Monster had some and they all parked right there, and they went inside and they got somebody to dance with them and they all danced with all their kids."

Mick "I have another question, you had names for others, now you're telling me, that Devil and Monster come over, who would be coming?"

Layla "Monster by himself, there's like four people with them, and he makes five, and then there's more, three and then two, and then another one, and then Shelly and then another one with her...that's pretty much it. "

Mick "When the bad stuff happens?"

Layla "It happens sometimes, Wednesday, Thursday, Friday, and when it's not those days, they come over and dance or have dinner, or have a movie, pretty much like a long thing, then we're at school. Annie has a babysitter, and she really does. When she went to pre-school, Devil was with Monster...."

Mick "Okay, about the people. You told me about Monster, you said he touched your privates now, when you name off these people, who out of all these characters have touched you?" (the girls had set up about 8 characters with their play people)

Lili " they guard, they rotate, and they all rotate. " Layla motions to the characters taking turns hurting the children.

Mick "What do you mean rotate?

Layla "One comes in and then another and another and another and another, what they do they take turns going over what they do. They, one goes in and does it and then one comes in and does it." (Again, she has the characters in her hand, showing them placing their bodies on a child, and pushing in their crotch area into them.)

Mick "what are they doing?.."

Layla "Just like Monster, (gestures with her hand, like "you know what I mean", they come and then three other ones come in, and they all go home and then three more come"

Mick "and where are your sisters?

Layla "my sisters are right here, and they come back, and then they do it again....three come and do it..."

Mick "what does that mean when three of them come and do it....."

Layla "this is me and this is Emily and this is Annie.....they come in and looks at them ,and see how they did it, and then they do it over again...like what Monster does....and so he does that....so he watches, to make sure they're doing it right.

Mick "and who are these people?..."

Layla  "I named them in the first part...they all go in and do it....this guy checks our privates".....(motions with the dolls as a character checks on each little girls insides)

Mick  "and what does that mean?........

Layla  " this is like this guy knocks on the door, I'm your new helper and Monster said this could be a problem, this is Layla, Emily and Annie...Layla, Emily and Annie....(acts as though she is introducing them to someone) these are new people...John Haden, this is all the rest of the guys, are the guys who were really there...and Ernie....Ernie is his uncle is a police, and he drives a police car over by, he goes over there, so if Monster got arrested, if he got killed, if he got in jail, he gets him out of a jail, more like of a favor, and um more of the people come and do it again, and they go over there, and then he does it again, and then they go like this, and then they keep on rotating, and one goes back and they go back out. These guys go back in and these guys go back out. And Mommy's sleeping.....everyday they rotate.......its like um we're its a busy street, and they don't bring their cars, Shelly, Mommy, Monster brings their cars.....she usually goes over to the neighbors and asks them if she could park down there, and then the neighbors say yes and they all park and the next day, we all go to bed and then they all come back. The next day they all come back, the guys, well, the guy that always comes back is Monster ...was lying down and he waked up and he hurts us the most, but the last day he wanted to go find more people to help him to rotate, he can't do it everyday he'd get tired, he wanted to get more friends, the people who come the most and there's only one girl, those five, Monster, Alec, he's his brother in the first part, they're twins, Alec, and her name Wheely, is Mom called her Wheely, and they have twins ya know......they do....."

Mick "who has twins?....."

Layla...."there's a girl......the guys are gone...pretend they're not there, she comes over and she has a broom, and twists it around and puts in our mouth....."

Mick  "a broom?"

Layla  " What is like a broom....."

Mick  "why would she put it in your mouth?"

Layla  "I don't know......and then like um and then she goes to get Monster, cause he knows, you know what he does...and Monster's uncle Ernie, and then Ernie does what Monster does. And then Ernie is kind of looks like Monster, he's a little bit, but he has a moustache, its white, he has police clothes, but its his car, its white on the front, and has black and its white and black, he has a different police car, he has a go cart at his house, cause people think he's a different cop and they know its Ernie, so they think Ernie drives a police car in Florida, and he comes down here too.....Florida is not that far, they take planes down there, Monster lives down there and he takes a plane and then they come back. The planes are at Florida and they take to Florida and then when they come back, Monster and Ernie and all these guys, take the plane,"

Mick  " I'm just kind of blown away by all this....I'm done, you did a good job trying to describe this.........."

Emily. (Layla's identical twin)

Emily  "This story is about Martha and she died because Monster came over and killed her and set her on fire, and then he, there was a playground out back and he set that on fire too, and then he went back home and went in the car and got Layla and Emily and Annie out of the car, and made them, they all got out and they weren't happy about it, and he said "don't tell your Dad" and we were going to and we didn't tell him about it, and then we all went home and now......"

(Emily was very anxious.)

Mick  "describe at Mommy's house whatever happens Layla and you wanted to tell me a story, so we got these little guys out and you can pick which ones to use to tell your story. Okay? That's Mommy.........who else do we have?....."

Emily  "They're all  coming in and getting and they're all watching them, and there's a cop they're helping Ernie too, "

Mick "and who are those two..."

Emily "these two are Mommy and John.....John Haden"

Mick "Does John Haden hurt you?"

Emily "No only Corey...."

Mick "how many of these people have touched your chachi? And who, I see how you have these people here, and you have Mommy, tell me what you want to tell me,"

Emily "they're getting where they're supposed to be, so Monster shows them with some dolls and they practice on some dolls too, and they get behind the dolls and we all have to go to where they went out to Mom's house and Monster had to pee in us and they all go where they're supposed to go, and Monster knows where he's supposed to go already. Monster went out and picked her up and then he hurt Annie's chachi's and then he got Layla and hurt her and then he grabbed Emily and did that to her too. He put his glove on and then he put his hand in her chachis and hurted it."

Mick "Who are these other people here? Any names?"

Emily "Not a bunch."

Mick "Any name would help? Who hurts you?"

Emily "Quincy, and John, and that's about it. That's who hurts me. And John Haden....and Monster....that's it.....and the rest guard."

Mick "Who is guarding, What does that mean?"

Emily "They guard the house and if any cops come they hide somewhere....he hides under the table...."

Mick "why would cops come?"

Emily "they'd come in....and um they have they look around the house, and they saw that someone was not in bed, Annie was in the bathroom. "

Mick "Who's on guard? Do you know any of these people?"

Emily "This one is I can't remember all their names..."

Mick "why doesn't Mommy know this?"

Emily "Mommy is asleep and if we yell everyone hides...Gramma is away...they all hide.......yea because they hear a bunch of noise"

Mick "how do they not see these guys? They're right there Emily"

Emily  "he got busted that one time Monster was being mad....."

Mick  "you did a pretty good job. Do you want someone to help you."

Emily  "Sure....."

Mick  "do you still want to go home." (the girls did not want to go home because they always knew Monster was there and they knew he was taking them away this time)

Emily  " No. "

Mick  "I'm trying to help you. Okay. I'm trying to help you that's why I'm doing this.  Okay. You don't deserve for this to happen to you. I want someone to help us. You wanted the judge to help you, and we had Dr. Judy help us.  (The psychologist was Dr. Judy.) What would you say honey?"

Emily  "I'd say Help us....."

Mick  "This is your chance."

Emily  (barely audible)  "I'd say help. We need help.  Help."

Mick  "Okay Emily...."

Annie, the youngest, then four years old

Annie

Mick  "What's going on.....who are these characters here. (with the toys)

"This is where my sister, is and here's Monster putting his pee pee in her"....(shows toys putting something in the little ones).....then he puts you back in your bed"

Mick  "where does he take you,"

Annie  "in the living room......"

Mick  "what does he do?"

Annie  "he puts his penis in the chachi...and other guys. They didn't even tell me their names so I don't know....know...."

Mick  "does anybody else or he is usually by himself....yea okay....what would you want to tell the judge"

Annie "that I'd want to tell the judge that Marfa and me are hurt by Monster, and then I'm going to tell the judge that Monster hurt a girl named Marfa and she's really nice, she had a playset, and that Monster burned down her house and set her bed on fire, fire, .........and he setted her on fire...(She stops speaking and looks into the distance, amazed at what she just said) ..Marfa had a playset, and she had a play set.....for real, in the backyard, and I looked in the back and I saw a play set and its really real."

Mick "You're really strong for talking about this, I'm trying to help. I want you to get help from somebody, and that's what we're doing."

Annie "That's the end of this story...that's my story...."

The End.

Now mind you, I realize this is not testimony, nor is this definitive. But these are little girls, throwing out very scary stories, about a sex offender, that their mother has made clear to everyone, she wants in their lives. He is a sex offender. A sex offender ordered to have no contact with these very little children. That in itself says the entire story. Sex offenders do not belong around children. Let me repeat that. Sex offenders do not belong anywhere near children.

And these little girls are terrified. They're telling terrible stories full of heartache and pain. And they have shown rape injuries, that have been testified to by an emergency room head physician of over 25 years. These little girls are pleading for help. They are babies really. At the time this DVD was made, the twins were six and the baby was four. Who tells stories like this? And these girls tell these stories to us, especially their Daddy, all the time.......pleading for help all the time. After their initial outburst two years previously, the stories are constant, and they are terrible. Little girls should have no reference for any type of story like these. (They would say to their Daddy "Monster pulls on his penis and puts it us until the white stuff comes out".......what little girl says that?)

And keep in mind, that the girls never say "Daddy, what are you talking about? Or, "Daddy what do you mean?" Or, "Daddy, Monster would never hurt us, you're silly." No, its always the same. Pain, suffering, penis, chachi, sex offender, fear, horrors, always the same. And they're on a tape saying all of this. And the judge did not care. She dismissed it as tho it was nothing. It floored me. It stunned me into complete oblivion. No little girls should ever together, as three sisters, be revealing the same horror stories, about the same man, who is a sex offender, who is court ordered to have no contact, who has sent them to the emergency room with rape injuries, and who has been testified against by the head of the emergency room of twenty five years, and by the court appointed psychologist. Has the judge lost her mind? Has she been paid off? The insanity is deafening. The horrors are blinding.

The judge refuses to hear any of their pain. She dismisses all of it. That is why it was so difficult to turn the dvd over to Devil's attorney. It was taped as a plea to the court, to the judge. To be heard by someone who would care about little girls hell. We didn't intend it as anything other than a plea from little girls for someone, anyone to listen to their pain. Big fat Mother Devil's lawyer, Grodey, goaded my son into turning over the dvd. Again, Mick had a moment of "she'll see their pain, she'll care." Again, we had that stupid belief in us. That someone would care.....nope. Don't care. Remember Richard Pryor, don't forget it. There's no Justice. It's Just us. And we don't care.........and sadly, its the truth. Where this judge got the idea that anyone coached anyone to say anything, or that anyone said this as some sort of a ploy; is frankly such insanity, I wonder what the hell kind of a life she's lived. As I've said repeatedly, if I were going to coach my granddaughters, or make up lies, I would say they were models, or actresses, or brilliant. I wouldn't make up horror stories of sexual abuse. And then by complete shock, the man doing it, would turn out to be a sex offender. What are the odds? What are the odds? If it looks like a duck, quacks like a duck, and walks like a duck.......maybe its a duck. If it been convicted (adjudicated) as a sex offender (96JD118), looks like a sex offender, talks like a sex offender and acts like a sex offender........bingo.....sex offender. And lets never ever forget, the one creature in this world, that can never be

156

changed, modified, turned into another beast........sex offender. Once a sex offender, always a sex offender. And this one was a sex offender in his teens. To a little one. A baby. No fear that it was a 17 year old with a 16 year old. No. A 17 year old with a baby. 96JD118. 96JD118. Look it up. Read it. Horrors. Horrors.

This was meant to be a plea to the judge to open an avenue, and get her to speak to the children. To hear their pleas. Not to be. I don't give a damn who you are, this outburst of insanity, from little girls should let anyone, anyone know, that something is very wrong.

As it turned out, no one cared. No one then. No one now. It is the saddest commentary on child abuse that I have ever heard.

I'm sure there are more. I'm sure that this is not the only story of hell upon children.

I pray that somehow, someway, this hell changes for my girls, and for other little children.

It's a hell no child should ever face.

As an interesting aside, I found this on the Texas governor's website, concerning child sexual abuse upon children.

The following two paragraphs I found on the Texas Governor's website: his plea for people to be diligent in cases of child sexual assault:

It is extremely difficult for a child to report sexual abuse. A very young child may not understand that what has happened is not normal or accepted.

More importantly, the abuser almost always discourages the child from telling anyone about the abuse. The strategies for silencing a sexual abuse victim are as ruthless as they are varied. The abuser may be someone whom the child depends upon and trusts; s/he may use the child's dependency and affection to extort a promise of secrecy. A more brutal perpetrator may threaten to harm (threatened to kill their Daddy and me) and even kill the child or other family members (killed Martha) or pets. Or the abuser may tell the child that the family will be broken up, the child blamed, or the child taken away from home if the secret becomes known. These are not altogether unrealistic fears for the child, unfortunately.

For many people, an allegation or disclosure of sexual abuse is indeed hard to accept. This is particularly true when the perpetrator is a family member or an otherwise law-abiding, respectable, and seemingly "nice," "normal" person. Many adults have a tendency to overlook, discount, minimize, explain away, or simply disbelieve allegations of sexual abuse. Yet children rarely lie or invent stories on their own about being sexually abused. The fact that children can sometimes be manipulated or coached should not dissuade anyone from reporting a child's revelation of sexual abuse. All responsible adults, but particularly those who work with children, should be aware that sexual abuse occurs and should be alert for the opportunity to aid a child who attempts to disclose abuse. The child's need for support and protection must come first.

Welcome to my nightmare. The lights are on, and nobody's home. I am horrified that the judge was as ignorant and uncaring as she was. To say that we were floored and stunned, is an understatement.

From the police, to the FBI (the agent in Illinois actually told my son after a meeting, in private, that she totally believed everything he was saying, but that her hands were tied, and she could not help him), to the courts, the representative, newspaper columnists, (one of them actually told me he couldn't corroborate my story, yet I have two notebooks full of all of the testimony and hospital records), judges (who knew the mother was a liar, and stated so), ..........no one came to the aid of three little girls. I did not include a lot of the interaction between police officers, the FBI, the state representative, or other government entities, because frankly they were so ignorant and beyond sanity, that I can barely remember them, much less write them down. Our time in court and with many legal authorities spanned over three years. I have included the most memorable and deafening that I can beat to actually recall. To recall all of it, and go through all of the

158

insanity, would kill me. I don't like to be overly melodramatic, but I did indeed suffer a heart attack at the peak of this hell. And all of it is insane. Nothing ever made sense. Hell. Pure hell.

This horror can never be changed for these little girls. I hope they survive their hell. I hope that their hearts can mend. I hope that their bodies survive. I pray that their little psyches can make it through. I pray that I see them again before I die, as does my mother who is now 86 years old. I pray that the hell that is played out on children in this country, becomes something that is addressed, and that their offenders rightfully go to jail. And that those who allow it to go on, that they lose their jobs, and suffer from the hell they refuse to stop. And that this country is enlightened to the pain and suffering of little ones, and that they become engaged and enraged to change the system. For the safety of little ones.

For Devil's family and friends. I pity you. I am saddened that anyone could be as ignorant and/or deceitful as all of you are to little children. I pray that you all get some professional help. And that you never have the opportunity to touch another child's life.

As a very strange, sad aside, we did indeed find out, about a month ago, that the mother Devil, works at the school that the girls attend. Staying close to her investments. In Conroe, Texas, Grice Elementary. I contacted the school when I saw pictures of Devil laying across a group of people on the school's internet page. Yes, she was laying across a group of women. The women were sitting side by side, about four of them, and she was lying across them, grinning like a fool. Like she was in a sorority fun night, or in a bar drinking with friends. Like she was 18 years old and they were her bitches. This woman has no class. No decency. No decorum. I think that fact has already been readily shown throughout my book.

I sent Grice Elementary principal, and school police officer (yes each school in Conroe, Texas, has a police officer. Why I don't know. He doesn't seem to care about child trafficking. ) I wanted to let them know that as mandated reporters, the girls were indeed in their school, against court orders, having been trafficked there, by their mother, and her sex offender boyfriend. And as an employee of the school, Devil to me, brought certain liabilities to the school. To me, having her employed by the school, was a certain thought process by other parents, that she had been vetted and that she was a decent, competent person. Other parents, could possibly allow their children, little children, (let's remember, 10 years old and 8 years old,) to possibly go to the home of Layla, Emily and Annie with the belief that they were safe. And in going to her home, they could readily be subjected to a sex offender, because Devil has always subjected her children to the sex offender. Lied for the sex offender, repeatedly. I see this as a very real threat to other children. Devil Mazur is an apologist, a supplier, a liar, a fool, for a sex offender. I think Monster must have moments of hysteria, where he is doubled over in laughter at the bounty he has landed upon with Devil and her ignorant family. Serving them up. Serving those little girls up faster than a whore can serve up the goods. Their ignorance has now, and always been the most amazing facet of this entire hell. Just deafening ignorance.

The way that this was handled: Get ready for this one. This is par for the course for the hell and stupidity we have faced throughout. The principal called the policeman and told him that she could not handle this. Devil worked for her, and she could not handle anything regarding this. A principal. A mandated reporter. Her greatest liability is to her students. Not to an employee who is trafficking her kids. Maybe its time for Devil to become the latest employee who is terminated. Maybe a sex trafficking mother doesn't belong in an elementary school as an employee. Just thinking.....again the nuts are running the asylum. Don't doubt it for a second. We have had the privelege of meeting and dealing with the most insane people in their professions. From school teachers, to principals, to police, to judges, to representatives......the lights are on, and no one is home.

So the policeman told me not to contact the principal again. She couldn't handle it. To only contact him. Now why he said this I don't know either. Mandated reporters.........mandated......reporters. A school principal is a mandated reporter. Someone who should be able and willing to KNOW something important regarding an employee in her school.

160

If not, and she is incapable of doing so, then her next stint may be disability. The inability to handle her position because of mental issues? Either take the bull by the horns, or go home. Sorry, time to put on your big girl panties. Grow up.

I went to work. Thought about it all day. I'm a certified nursing assistant. I too am a mandated reporter. If I become aware that one of my residents is being abused, hurt, threatened, harmed in any way, by anyone, I am mandated, MANDATED, to report that person. Then my facility is mandated to do an investigation. The person who is being investigated is put on temporary leave, until the charges can be determined. Mandated. There are many of us who are mandated reporters. (And a school principal is one of them. Calling in "I can't handle this, make her stop", is not even close to admissable. Refusing to do her job! Turn in your resignation, turn in your time sheets, and go home. Do not pass go. Do not collect $200. Go directly to jail.) So I came home and emailed both of them. I basically said "You both are mandated reporters. Your actions and your statements are both in total contrast to what should be done. I know as a mandated reporter, I do not have a choice. I am required to make the charge and the facility must investigate."

They both, along with their school board president, blocked me from emailing them.

Kill the messenger. Kill the messenger.

And we wonder why these horrific situations in this world are allowed to happen? Because educated people who should know better, refuse to do the right thing. Educated people acting like idiots. For a woman who is trafficking her children to a sex offender. The insanity is deafening. Devil and Monster must just have laughing fits at the bounty of stupidity that they has been graced upon them.

Kill the messenger. Kill the messenger.

And I ask, as you read this, try, try to watch a movie about rape. Not even child rape. A young woman being raped. I have tried. I will be going through the channels, and see a movie about rape. I happened onto a movie "I Know Who Killed Me" recently on a Sunday afternoon. I tried to watch this movie for only a few minutes. The young lady portraying the rape victim was Lindsay Lohan, I would guess at about 20 some years of age. I happened onto the movie, which was a scene that was actual victimization and violence against this beautiful young woman, and I had to stop watching. So as you read this, think, really think, of an innocent little child, little girl, tiny little girls, being forced to do such horrid things. Being hit, being raped, being forced to perform oral sex, being forced to perform anal sex, being tortured, being scared, being blindfolded, being toyed with as their molesters laugh, watching their sisters being victimized, being victimized themselves. Think of yourself at the ages of 1, up until nine and ten years of age. Your memories of childhood. Facing this. Dealing with this. Being raped. By savages.

Before I was a party to this hell, upon my own granddaughters, it is something I had never even imagined. It is a hell beyond anything I have been able to comprehend. Now, be a little girl. A baby, two years old, five years old, seven years old...........and no one ever comes to your side to help you. Comprehend that for just a moment. This is the life my granddaughters live, everyday. Everyday, every minute, of their little lives.

The behaviors, the attitudes, the thought processes, the actions, the horrors, the insanity, the depravity, the absolute hell, that has been played out by Devil and Monster and their families and friends upon my granddaughters, is more hell that I ever dreamed I would or could encounter in this life. And to know that my granddaughters, little girls, have had this as their childhoods, is just deafening in its scope. I cannot begin to related to you the number of sleepless nights, nightmares, hysterical crying, and heart broken days I have spent. I went through at least six months where I could not begin to fall asleep. My dreams became nightmares of hell that I prayed I would forget as soon as I awoke. I know their father has suffered tremendously with the same hell. All of us have.

I end with a prayer.

162

Dear God, let little children be safe and know that they are loved and honored. Let the sex offenders who hurt children and their defenders pay for what they have done to little ones. Let the world realize that this cannot go on. This has to end. It is abhorrent and needs to be stopped. Someone, somewhere......help little children in this hell. Amen.

I love you Layla, Emily and Annie. I wait for the day when I get to see you again. Safe. Out of your hell. You are strong, amazing, brave little girls, who tried as hard as anyone could at your tender age to fight for yourselves, and actually believed that someone might help you. You did nothing wrong. All of those around you, who should have helped you, should be ashamed of themselves. I love you always. Always and forever.

Love, Mim

# And in the end...

I am left with so much anguish and pain. Little girls lost. Just sent off into Neverland and banished to a sex offender, who terrorizes them and rapes them, with the consent of the mother and her awful friends and family.

I try and try to have a heart and believe, but its so hard, when I know everyday they are destroyed a little further, hurt a little more, damaged a little more, by their very own mother.

Wondering where their Daddy is. When will someone help them. They had begged their Daddy to kill the Molester and Mommy used those words against him, instead of helping her babies.

The little girls are left to two vicious adults who are willing to terrorize and destroy them. It is an abomination.

In the end, the courts, the stupid Judge K, decided that the father would have no visitation, and Monster could do and live wherever she wanted with the children.

So the children are doomed to this hell. They are doomed to live with the Monster who rapes them.

My son has no visitation rights, nor will the courts allow him any visitation. The lawyer Grodey said that he would fight my son if he tried to get visitation. Welcome to hell. The children are with the sex offender, across state lines, perpetrated by their mother, and her family, with no hope of any reconciliation with their father. Why? Because he tried to protect them from a sex offender who was court ordered to have no contact with them, but was and is with them all the time.

And in the end....the love you take, is equal to the love you make.

164

So for Monster and Devil.........you have been given the right to destroy the lives of three little children. It just so happens that these three little children, little girls, are my granddaughters, that I love more than anything in this world, and that I haven't seen in over two years.

I pray that one day this hell is stopped.

Please God, find a way to make it stop.

I love you girls. I pray for you everyday, that this will end.

I love you girls

this is the End

# Transcript of Doctor's Court Testimony

13th day of February 2009

Can you please state your name and spell your last name for the record?

My name is Dr. Ron Kruzak. First name R-o-n. Last name is K-r-u-z-a-k.

Doctor do you currently have, are you currently licensed to practice medicine in the state of Illinois?

Yes.

And how long have you been so licensed?

Since 1983.

Mr. Grodey, lawyer for Devil:

I'm just gonna stipulate to the curriculum vitae, and he can be found to be an expert in the field of medicine, if we want to speed this up.

The father, Mick's lawyer:

Q. Dr. how long have you been practicing in the emergency room?

A. Since I finished my residency in 1983.

Q. Okay, are you board certified?

A. Yes.

Q. Do you have hospital privileges beside St. Mary's?

A. No, just St. Mary's.

Q. And you work in the hospital on a full time basis?

A. Yes, I've been the Director of the Emergency Department at St. Mary's Hospital.

Q. I am showing you what I've marked as Defendant's Exhibit No.3 for identification, do you recognize that document?

A. Yes I do.

Q. And what is it?

A. It is a copy of our report from December 2, 2007.

Q. And on that date did you treat a minor child in the emergency room?

A. Yes I treated a child named Emily Thomas.

Q. And she was brought in by her father?

A. That's correct.

Q. And did you make a diagnosis after examining the child?

A. Yes I did.

Mr. Grodey: Objection, foundation.

The Court: Sustained.

Q. Well what happened when the child came to the hospital?

A. We took a history, um from the father. And we performed a video--we did a physical exam and then a videotape of the genitalia called video colposcopy in conjunction with a nurse.

Q. Why did you do that?

A. We routinely do that in cases of suspected sexual abuse.

Q. And in this case was there - - how did you know- - how did you know there was suspected sexual abuse?

A. It was based on the history obtained from the child as well as the finding of a tear of the posterior fourchetta in exam.

Q. And what does a tear of the posterior fourchetta mean?

A. That basically means a tear of the vaginal opening and the rectum, which is a classic sign of forcible penetration.

Q. And you made this finding when?

A. During our exam of the child and during the video colposcopy.

Q. And on what date was this?

A. This was on December 02, of 07.

Q. Now, you had mentioned a history from both the parent and the child. You got - - what was the history you got from the child?

A. Well as I refer to my notes, from that date, I noted that the patient was here with her father. And I'm quoting from the record. Father states man named Monster Thomson, a convicted pedophile, is living in a house with his ex-wife and girls. Emily said, quote, he played with himself and Layla, end quote.

Then Layla, her sister, then said, quote, he played with himself and touched my chotchy, that's c h o t c h y, end quote. And then the child indicated that this was indicating to her vagina.

Q. When you put the words in quote, Doctor, what does that mean?

A. These are the exact words from the child.

Q. Do you have an opinion to a reasonable degree of medical certainty that the child that you examined was a victim of sexual abuse?

A. Yes.

Q. And what is that opinion?

A. That the child was a victim of abuse.

Q. And what do you base that on?

A. Based on the history from a five-year-old girl and the findings on examination- as I mentioned, a tear of the posterior fourchetta.

Q. And you - - did you notify DCFS?

A. Yes we did.

Q. Did you have any other involvement with this patient after that?

A. No.

Q. Were there any other significant findings from - - from the medical records that I showed you?

A. No.

Father's lawyer - - I have nothing further of this witness Judge.

Cross Examination:

Mr. Grodey - mother's lawyer

Q. All right. How often do you deal with, how often do you examine patients who have possible sexual injuries?

A. Several times a year. I'm the key physician responsible for doing sexual assault exams in our emergency department.

Q. Okay. Now , can you tell me again what the injury was that the minor child had?

A. Yes, the vaginal opening, there was a tear at the bottom. So, if a woman is in the position for a Pap smear, laying on her back, that area, the bottom of the vaginal opening, towards the rectum, that part of the vaginal opening had a tear in the midline.

Q. Okay. So that would be - - and correct me if I'm wrong. And I don't mean to be too graphic here. But obviously, we're in a courtroom here, trying to describe this. You've got a vaginal opening. And then you have, you know, obviously, further underneath you have a rectal opening.

A. Mmm - hmm. Yes.

Q. And this is the area between the two of them at the bottom of the vaginal opening you're saying had the tear?

A. No, not between the two. Actually, its part of the vaginal opening itself.

Q. Okay.

A. Okay? Vag - -

Q. But at the bottom on the outside of the vaginal- -

A. Correct.

Q. And you're saying that this is indicative of a sexual act by somebody else on this minor child?

A. Yes. It's indicative of forcible penetration.

Q. Okay. Is it indicative of anything else?

A. Um, not that I know of.

170

Q. Okay.

A. It's indicative of forcible penetration.

Q. So you're saying that the only way that a person can get a tear on the bottom of their vagina is by forcible penetration?

A. Forcible penetration by any object which would cause a tear - - or penis, what have you.

Q. Um, riding a bike couldn't do it or falling on something couldn't do that?

A. In twenty-five years of practice I've never seen that happen.

Q. Okay. Did you have - - I mean, did you take anything - - as far as - - well, did you do a rape kit on the minor child?

A. Yes.

Q. Okay. And did you get the results from the rape kit?

A. Those typically go to the state. The results we get would be any test of infectious disease, such a gonorrhea, chlamydia, et cetera.

Q. Did you get the results back?

A. Yes.

Q. And what are the results of those....

A. The results....

Q. - - - - - the tests?

A. - - - - from the gonorrhea and chlamydia tests were negative.

Q. Okay. .....and as far as the tear goes. Can you describe that to the Court?

A. Sure. It was a superficial tear, approximately four - - three to four millimeters of the midline of the posterior fourchetta of the vaginal introitus.

Q. Okay. Now, um, then - - we're talking three to four millimeters I guess - - what I want to do is have you help me to understand. This was - - is this on the very outside of the vagina? Is this - - you know somewhat on the inside of the vagina? Is it - - where is it at?

A. It's basically on the outside as you look at the vaginal opening.

Q. Uh - huh.

A. Okay? Basically, the - - inside the labia, that area right at the bottom, is where the posterior fourchetta is. It is basically the bottom of the vaginal opening, which we're seeing externally. And as we look at that area, you can see that there was a small tear - - and I probably should say more like three to five or six millimeters in length.

Q. Okay. Do you have these in your records as far as the tear?

A. No, but we have it documented in video.

Q. Okay. Do you have the video with you today?

A. I do not.

Q. So as far as the - size of the tear, the location of the tear, you're just going based on memory from the incident?

A. Yes.

Q. Okay.

A. But it, again documented in the video for - -

Q. Did you review that video before you came in today?

A. No I didn't.

Q. So, again, you're going off memory from something that happened a few years ago as far as the size of the tear, - - the position of the tear and everything you've testified to today?

A. Yes I remember it very clearly.

Q. Okay. And you do multiple cases like this a year?

A. I do.

Q. Um, and do you find it - - well, obviously, as part of your job as a doctor you - - you are taught to properly annotate things in your medical records when you're taking a history of a client - - or the patient. Is that correct?

A. Correct.

Q. Okay. And this isn't something that you would have normally annotated in your medical records as far as the size or the position of the tear?

A. We do in some cases. But, fortunately since we do the video colposcopy, that is the best record: because you see the actual video instead of writing something to try to describe something visually. Having the video tape is the best documentation.

Q. Okay. Now the conversation you spoke of having. You said that there was a history given to you by the child or by the father, was it?

A. Correct.

Q. Okay. Now the father was present the entire time of the examination?

A. Um, I don't recall a hundred percent if he was there during the exam. I believe he was but - - - -

Q. But the questioning you did of the child and him happened at the same time as far as the incident?

A. Um not necessarily. You know depending on the situation, we may have the parents step out of the room so that we can talk to the child without a parent there. It depends on the situation.

Q. Okay. As far as this case, do you recall whether of not dad stepped out of the room while you were taking to the child?

A. I don't recall specifically - - that --

Q. Okay. So - but your reports show that basically you were having a conversation with dad and the child at some point during the interview. But there's no indication that you ever had a conversation with the child by herself. Is that right?

A. Could you repeat that question, please?

Q. In your reports it shows that you have a conversation with the dad and the child.

A. Yes

Q. Correct? But there is no indication in your reports that you ever asked dad to step out of the room to have a conversation with the child? Is that right?

A. There is no documentation of that, correct.

Q. Now, most of the history that you had gotten based on the age of this child would have been from the father?

A. You're saying was that most of history was obtained from the father?

Q. The history and the information about Monster Thomson? Did that come from the father?

A. Well, the only information about Monster Thomson is what I record in the record.

Q. Okay. And that was that the father indicated that Monster Thomson was living with the mom and that he thought that Monster had vaginally penetrated the minor child? Is that right?

A. No. I'll read from the record once again to make sure its accurate. What I indicated in the record is patient with father. Father states man named Monster Thomson, a convicted pedophile is living in a home with his ex-wife and two girls.

Q. Okay. And then as far as the tear and - - or the discomfort in the vaginal area, did you talk to the minor child about the discomfort in the vaginal area?

A. Did I talk to her about the discomfort? I don't recall talking to her about any discomfort, but.....

Q. Okay. But you asked the child at one point how she got the tear.

A. Yes.

Q. And she said it was Monster Thomson?

A. Again, I'll quote my record. Emily said he made me watch while he played with himself and Layla. And then, again, Layla, her sister, said he played with himself and touched my chotchy, end quote.

Q. Okay. Now as far as the - - as far as the examination goes, you cannot tell what, if anything was placed in her vagina. Correct?

A. The tear indicates that something was forcibly inserted or forced to be inserted into her vaginal opening.

Q. Okay. But you don't know what that was. Correct?

A. No. I can't tell you what it was. But in any case - -

Q. You don't know who, if anybody, tried to force something into her vaginal area based on your medical examination. Correct?


A. Repeat that question please.

Q. You don't know who if anybody tried to force something into her vaginal area based on your medical examination. Correct?

A. Based on my questioning on and her response, with a reasonable degree of certainty I can say that this person as she referred to was the one who touched her chotchy as she said, and inserted something.

Mr. Grodey:

I'd object to that answer and move to strike as to a reason reasonable degree of certainty. I don't think that he's been - - anything has given him, as far as the qualifications that have been stipulated to, given him the ability to give a reasonable degree of certainty as to the statements of the child being correct.

The Court:

I'm not gonna strike it. I'm gonna take it for what it has - - is worth with regards to what is and is not a medical diagnosis or statement. He's talking - - I mean we're talking apples and oranges here.

By Mr. Grodey:

Q. Okay. Um now, it is possible that this tear came from something other than a penis being inserted in her vagina. Is that correct?

A. Yes, it could be an object.

Q. And you don't know sitting here today what, if anything, was inserted into her?

176

Father's attorney: Objection

Q. - - vagina, correct?

Father's attorney: Asked and answered, Judge.

The Court: Excuse me?

Father's attorney - Asked and answered.

The Court: Sustained

By Mr. Grodey:

Q. With the exception of the tear, was there anything that you found that suggest - - with the exception also of the conversations that you had, was there anything that you found that indicated any type of sexual contact between the minor child and anybody else?

A. Yes. The other thing is what the child told us.

Q. Okay. And what I said was with the exception of what the child said, and the tear, was there anything else that you found to indicate that the child had been sexually abused?

A. Well, a third thing, again, would be the history from the father. But other than that, no.

Q. Okay - and this history that you gave us, is again - - well, you know, strike that.

When you do an examination of the minor child - - well, tell me how - - tell me how you do the sexual examination. Tell me how the procedure is - - is done - - from front to end.

A. Okay. We have a specific room for doing this where we have all the equipment for video colposcopy. We have the child lie in the most comfortable position, which usually on her back. A nurse assists. And then we take a look at the external genitalia. We start the video colposcopy. We make sure to put the name in the field of vision so that there's no question about who this person is in the video. And then we gently spread the labia and look for any signs of trauma, bruising, tears, lacerations, et cetera. And we videotape this.

And we obtain cultures which means putting swabs in for GC and chlamydia culture. Um, and also get a culture for - - it's called a wet mount for trichomoniasis and fungus, or yeast. And then we also look at the rectum for any tears or lacerations. And that's pretty much it.

Q. Okay. So as part of your - - - part of your examination, you actually stick items into the vaginal are of the child as well. Is that correct?

A. We put swabs in.

Q. Is that done by you, or is it done by a nurse, prior to you - -

A. By me.

Q. - - the child? Did you take the history, um, from the child and the father prior to the actual medical examination?

A. Yes.

Q. And obviously you only do these type of examinations, um - - well, strike that.

The - - the - - I guess the whole gist of this - - of this is that you, being a person who specializes in these sexual examinations, you were called in to do this case especially because of the sexual implications?

A. Typically, these are scheduled when I work. So between DCFS and KC Casa, they schedule this with me, and one of our key nurses who are trained to do this on days when I'm working.

Q. Okay. And this was one that was scheduled prior to you - -

A. That I don't recall. It may have been scheduled, or she may have just come in when I was working.

Q. But based on the medical - - or the history that was given to you by the father and the child, you treated this as a sexual case right off the bat?

A. Sexual assault, yes.

Q. So I mean, your - - your - - based on what you're told by the father and the child, would you say you were - - you obviously were looking for the things to show that were was was a sexual attack or the child or a sexual molestation of the child?

A. We're there to take a complete history and physical The nurse usually evaluates the child first and then passes the information on to us. And then we do the history and physical to determine what the medical conditions are.

Q. Now, you don't have that video with you today. But can - - I mean, can you tell me how you went through the examination and exactly what you found as you were going through the examination step by step?

A. Sure, again, as I mentioned, we look at the external genitalia first. We have a child laying on her back. The nurses will - -

Q. I'm sorry. Let me just stop you for a second. I'm not talking about in general. I'm talking about this specific case right here.

A. Mmm hmm. That's what I'm talking about.

Q. Okay.

A. I do every case the same essentially. So the child is laying on her back. The nurse holds the legs open. We look at the external genitalia, vulva, et cetera. We then, with gentle pressure, separate the labia and look at the vaginal intoitrus. We videotape this as we're doing it. And we look, as I mentioned. For any signs of discharge or trauma.

We then take a swab for chlamydia, gonorrhea, also Trichomoniasis, and fungus. And again, we then - - when we're done with the examination of the vaginal area, we then look at the rectum for any tears - - or trauma. And then when we're done, we turn off the videotape.

Actually, after that - - well, before doing the physical exam, we also look for any signs of abuse on the skin, bruising, et cetera - - which could be due to physical abuse.

Q. Did you see any of that in this instance?

A. I don't have any documented, no.

Q. Now, the videotape, is that available? I mean is that something you still have it preserved and - -

A. We typically keep that in our medical records.

Q. And you didn't bring that with you today?

A. I was not asked to bring that.

Q. And this procedure that you're talking about to the Court, this is a procedure that you use every time. So that's why you're describing how you - - how you do it from front to end. You do the same procedure every time.

A. Correct.

Q. Did you have any idea how long the child was in the custody of the father before the father brought the child to you?

A. No, I do not.

Q. Do you have any idea of the - - strike that.

Q. Was there any semen found in our around the child as far as her vaginal area?

A. That's something that is tested by the State in their forensic kit.

Q. Did the state also test her?

A. We sent the materials and the kit to the State. And then the State does their analysis, which - - all the things that include - - which I do not have a list of.

Q. It would be safe to say that - - pretty - - that would be pretty important to see those types of results. I mean, if you're gonna find out if she was raped or not, if there was semen present and that type of stuff, it would be important to see those results from State as well?

Father's lawyer:

Objection Judge, to the form of the question.

The Court: Overruled

The Witness: Okay. So you're asking is the finding of semen important?

By Mr. Grodey:

Q. Well, no. I'm asking if the finding of the - - all the - - the test kit, the State rape kit that you're talking about. If the findings from that kit would be important also in looking at whether or not the child was raped -- or was molested?

A. I think its, you know additional data. But based on the data we have here, you know, that would be additional, but not necessary.

Q. Okay. And one last question for you. The - - the tear that we've been talking about here the entire time does it - - in every instance is that type of a tear produced from sexual assault?

A. In my experience of research of - - reading about sexual abuse, taking care of children, um, you know, there are certain things which are called classic or pathopnemonic findings of sexual abuse. This is one of those pathopnemonic findings of sexual abuse in a child.

Q. Okay. But - - and I understand that being a sign of abuse on a child. But in every instance does a tear as we've described here today mean that sexual abuse has occurred to that minor child?

Father's lawyer: Objection. Asked and answered, Judge.

The Court: Overruled.

The Witness: Could you repeat the question again?

By Father's lawyer:

Q. I understand what all the research goes to and what you've studied and what you've seen in your experience. But in every instance does a vaginal tear, as described here today. does it always come from sexual contact?

Father's counsel: Judge I'd just object to the - - to the question. Sexual abuse or sexual contact can be - - come in different forms. And I believe he's trying to limit the witness in a specific area; therefore almost trying to get him to define those terms.

The Court: This is a bench trial, and that's not a specific objection. I'm gonna overrule it. He can answer the question if he can.

The Witness: Um, I would have to look at the research and see if there are any cases that specifically say that a tear of the posterior fourchetta can be caused by other instances. I mean, you have tears, you know, of other areas of the vaginal area, like say from

182

bicycle things. But that may be a tear which, different than where this is located and what it looks like.

By Mr. Grodey:

Q. But this tear - - I mean, this tear that we've talking about here is caused by something being forced into the vagina?

A. Yes.

Q. Bottom line?

A. Yes.

Q. And it can be caused by anything being forced into the vagina. Correct?

A. It would have to be caused by an object large enough to stretch that tissue and cause a tear.

Q. Okay. And now deep was this cut - - that is tear?

A. Again, it was superficial. It did not require suturing, but it was a tear of the skin, which shaved the underlying submucosa or the - -

Q. Okay. Could this also be scratches from something? Could it be a fingernail? Could it be something other than a penis being pushed in?

A. Okay. Well, that's really several questions. Could it be a scratch? No. It did not have the appearance of a scratch. And then your other question, could it be something other than a penis. And I think I already answered that, that it could be caused by any object large enough to stretch the skin to cause a tear.

Whereupon there was a brief interruption.

Mr. Grodey: That's all I have.

The Court: I have a question, which is this. Did you conduct the - - did you personally obtain the history or did someone in your employ or under - - at your direction obtain the history?

The Witness: I did.

The Court: Okay. father's counsel , do you have any questions?

Redirect Examination

Q. Doctor, why is it that you - - you testified on cross examination that you remembered this case. Why is that?

A. Because this is one of the few cases where I've seen that classic, you know. superficial laceration of the posterior fourchetta. So that was very memorable.

Mick's attorney: Nothing further Judge.

Mr. Grodey: I don't have anything based on that.

The Court: Thank you, Doctor. You may step down.

As a very sad aside, this should have been the end. The judge who ordered a no contact order against the Monster Thomson, to never be with, live with, have any contact with the children, listened to an emergency room physician of 25 years, the head emergency room doctor, testify to rape injuries upon five year old twins, did nothing to protect them. Nothing. We have been thrown into hell. These little girls have been thrown into the pits of hell. And we along with them.

# My Prayer for My Beautiful Girls

I Believe in You
Though I don't have any idea what to do
I stop, I pray
I pray for a day
When Your Monster mother will know
That her Molester she has chosen to love
(How can she even know what love is)
Is in fact tearing your world apart
Maybe she already knows
But doesn't care, obviously
The pain, the fear, the horror that
Has become your life
Three beautiful little angels
Handed to the Molester
By their mother, who is a Monster/Devil
The mother and the rapist both Monsters,
Their own mother
Their own birth mother
The revulsion I feel is so abhorrent
I can barely comprehend
I can barely think anyway
I pray. I pray.
I stop. I pray.
I pray for little girls who
Have Monster for a mother
Or as little Annie says SCARY MOMMY
And yet this Scary Mommy
Has fits if
Someone questions the fact
That her own mother
Her own mother
Who along with Devil serves up the children
That her own mother who claims she was once raped
Has no heart to save her babies from a Molester
Save her own babies from a Molester
How could someone not believe little girls

Little girls pleading for help
Little girls with rape injuries on their tiny bodies
With bravery and strength beyond their years
Pleading with my son, myself, and anyone will who listen
To help them
They say
"He pees on me, he puts his hands in my chachi,
He kisses me with his tongue, and wants my tongue in his mouth,
He has me rub his chachi, til he pees
He puts me outside with no clothes on, til I cry,
He takes me out of bed when I'm sleeping and rubs me naked,
He scratches my chachi with his fingernails,
It hurts, it hurts, it hurts
I want it to stop
He makes me stop crying so no one will hear
He puts tape on my mouth so I can't cry out loud
No noise, no noise, no noise,
He says bad words,
He scares me
He scares me
He scares me"
Maybe Scary Mommy, Shorn and Monster will one day
Burn in Hell
For the horror and pain they have willfully inflicted upon
Three little girls
Three little girls
Three little girls
Who wanted to do nothing more than be loved
The harshness, the stupidity, the horror
The sadness
Inflicted upon little girls
Inflicted upon little girls
Showering them in pain, showering them in fear,
And feeling no guilt,
While pain is inflicted
Upon
Three Beautiful Little girls
Three beautiful sweet little girls
These beautiful, sweet darling, little girls

At the time all of this was revealed
These little girls were 5 and 3
Little girls, twins 5 baby 3
The hell is rained down upon babies.
Babies in hell
Babies in hell
May God hear your voices
May God take the pain away
May God let Monster and Devil know
That you do not do this to
Three Beautiful Little Girls
I stop. I pray.
I stop. I pray.

# Epilogue

I remember well the feelings I had after the final court date. They were mostly of sadness. Sadness that the children's mother was a liar, and did not care about the danger she placed her children in. That she didn't love her children enough to protect them. That the children had sought help so many times, and no one listened. That the authorities had no heart for what was happening to the children. It was an intense sadness that enveloped me and continues to haunt me. I don't understand how no one helps.

And as I have been told repeatedly, it is local. If the local authorities won't help you, then tough. I have searched and searched and searched for help. And no one will lift a finger. I do not understand how the raping and trafficking of little girls is alright in this country. I do not understand it at all. Everyone argues about who I should contact, instead of digging in and stopping this hell upon little girls.

I suffered a heart attack about seven months after the girls left. I had struggled and struggled with their loss. I hurt. Everything in me hurt. My heart, my mind, my conscience, my body......I was in mourning for the loss of my babies. And when you know they are in danger and being hurt, you hurt for the pain they are in. I know that they are suffering, and it kills me.

I am further tortured by the fact that the Devil and Monster's families are all fine with the fact that they have lied and continue to place the children in harm's way, with no conscience to help them. When I discovered that they were all friends on facebook, the sex offender, and the grandmother, and the aunt, and the friends, I was stunned. The way they fixed that......took down their facebook accounts. So they could further hide the fact that the children were with the sex offender, against court order.

I had to have a test to find the cause of my heart attack. The tests showed no blockage and no physical damage. A broken heart. I had a broken heart. And I knew it. My heart ached for months.

I am now living with this heartache. I have learned to try and relax and not always be in stress. I hear their little voices, I see their little faces, and I melt.

I know my son has aged so much since they left. He hurts for them too. We all do.

I pray that one day the call of children being savaged and raped by a Monster will call all the authorities out and cause someone to come to their aid. Until that day, all I can do is pray and hope that a change comes about. Please someone, help me make that change.

I would also like to acknowledge my family, Joe, Beau, Mick, Teddy, Chloe, Diana, Janet and Wavel, whose support for me was unwavering, and who love these girls and want their hell to end, as I do. I am so thankful for my family.

God Bless.